Fighting Tax Crime – The Ten Global Principles, Second Edition

OECD

BETTER POLICIES FOR BETTER LIVES

This document, as well as any data and map included herein, are without prejudice to the status of or sovereignty over any territory, to the delimitation of international frontiers and boundaries and to the name of any territory, city or area.

The statistical data for Israel are supplied by and under the responsibility of the relevant Israeli authorities. The use of such data by the OECD is without prejudice to the status of the Golan Heights, East Jerusalem and Israeli settlements in the West Bank under the terms of international law.

Please cite this publication as:
OECD (2021), *Fighting Tax Crime – The Ten Global Principles, Second Edition*, OECD Publishing, Paris, *https://doi.org/10.1787/006a6512-en*.

ISBN 978-92-64-50360-1 (print)
ISBN 978-92-64-57287-4 (pdf)

Preface

As Chair of the OECD Task Force on Tax Crimes and Other Crimes (TFTC), I am honoured to present the second edition of *Fighting Tax Crime – The Ten Global Principles*. The new edition includes counter-strategies for tackling professionals who enable tax and other white collar crimes, successful case studies on recovering virtual assets (such as crypto-currencies) and best practices in international co-operation in the fight against tax crimes. It further compiles country reports of 33 jurisdictions, including 27 OECD members. All of these jurisdictions are working with the shared aim of the full global implementation of the Ten Global Principles, establishing a common tax enforcement and tax investigation standard to enhance international cooperation, and build trusted relationships between the organisations responsible for tax crime investigation. These Ten Global Principles are now complemented by the Tax Crime Investigation Maturity Model, allowing jurisdictions to self-evaluate to what extent the Ten Global Principles are implemented and practised in their domestic tax investigation branch, and providing them with a clear pathway to possible further improvements.

The TFTC, founded in 2010 as a successor to the small Sub-Group on Tax Crimes and Money Laundering, also deals with issues closely related to, and often intertwined with tax crime, such as money laundering, terrorism financing and corruption, as well as cross-cutting issues such as the "whole of government approach" set out in the OECD Oslo Dialogue. The list of reports published by the TFTC over the last ten years is impressive and these reports and other material relevant to the fight against tax crime and other crimes can be found on the OECD website.

For more than 20 years I have been the Head of the Strategic Anti-Fraud Division of the Federal Ministry of Finance in Austria, and I have to say that the creation of the TFTC, a unique body then and now, was a hugely important milestone in enhancing the international efforts to tackle tax crime and other crimes. I look back with pride on my involvement as in this group and its extensive work programme from the outset.

An outstanding achievement of the OECD's work in the enforcement area is connecting the fight against tax crimes with the fight against money laundering. The OECD Council Recommendations on tax measures for further combatting bribery of foreign officials in international business transactions, and to facilitate co-operation between tax and other law enforcement agencies to combat serious crimes, represent crucial steps for effective sharing of information between tax administrations, other law enforcement agencies and financial intelligence units. Furthermore, it is encouraging to see the OECD working on expanding international co-operation in the fight against tax crimes, including in the recovery and repatriation of assets that are derived of tax crimes.

For the future, I will take this opportunity to highlight three priority areas in particular.

First, the importance of supporting developing countries and their tax administrations in building capacity for successful tax crime investigations. In a world increasingly economically interlinked, economic and financial threats such as cross-border VAT and other forms of tax fraud, money laundering, corruption and illicit financial flows, affect all jurisdictions, both developed and developing. Furthermore, without a full range of instruments and capacities to fight tax crimes, developing countries may struggle to secure a more sustainable economic future. Consequently, the OECD International Academy for Tax and Financial Crime Investigation was launched in 2013 in Ostia, followed in the years between 2017 and 2019 by the establishment of regional centres for Africa in Nairobi, for Latin America in Buenos Aires and for Asia-Pacific in Tokyo. My sincere hope is that the Academy functions as a knowledge hub for all developing and developed countries, enabling them to better fight tax evasion and other tax crimes, including international tax schemes and illicit financial flows.

Second, we need to look closely at the effectiveness of current information sharing practices and policies. While it is, of course, of great importance to safeguard the confidentiality of taxpayer information, this can be an important source in risk assessing for tax crimes and money laundering. In particular, I believe we should look further at how the extensive information on financial accounts held by taxpayers outside of their jurisdiction of residence, that is now exchanged automatically under the OECD Common Reporting Standard, can also be accessed in a timely and efficient manner by financial intelligence units. There are, of course, a number of important issues to be considered, but I hope that the TFTC can help to build an evidence base of why the sharing of such information can be an important tool in tackling tax crime.

Third, and in a similar vein, I hope that the TFTC can also provide impetus to deliberations on the sharing of beneficial ownership information between criminal investigators, hopefully in closer to real-time. Many crimes are facilitated through shell companies which operate across multiple jurisdictions. Under traditional exchange of information request procedures, the time required to track such companies and understand the intricate linkages that can exist, can end up frustrating criminal investigations in some cases. In an interconnected world, where technology can achieve so much so quickly, this is an area where we can surely do better.

Finally, may I again commend to you the second edition of the Ten Global Principles, which should guide us and our partner administrations on how to work most effectively together in the fight against tax crime. Let's continue to collaborate, communicate and cooperate.

Herwig Heller

Chair 2019-2021, OECD – TFTC

Director of Anti-Fraud, Federal Ministry of Finance of Austria

Foreword

First published in 2017, *Fighting Tax Crime – The Ten Global Principles* is the world's first comprehensive guide to fighting tax crimes. Its ten essential principles cover the legal, institutional, administrative, and operational aspects necessary for putting in place an efficient system for fighting tax crimes and other financial crimes, while ensuring taxpayers' rights are respected. This second edition addresses new challenges, such as tackling professionals who enable tax and white-collar crimes, and fostering international co-operation in the recovery of assets. Drawing on the experience from jurisdictions in all continents, the report also highlights successful cases relating to virtual assets, complex investigations involving joint task forces, and the use of new technology tools to fight tax crimes and other financial crimes. Individual chapters accompany the report, where jurisdictions have benchmarked their domestic framework against the Ten Global Principles.

This document was prepared by the OECD Centre for Tax Policy and Administration (CTPA) and was approved by the OECD Task Force on Tax Crimes and Other Crimes and by the Committee on Fiscal Affairs. The data included in this document was submitted by and under the responsibility of the relevant authorities of each participating jurisdiction, and the Secretariat has not verified its accuracy. The second edition of this report was prepared by Marcos Roca of the OECD Secretariat under the supervision of Melissa Dejong and Peter Green. The authors are thankful to all participating jurisdictions who actively engaged in this project despite the constraints imposed by the COVID-19 pandemic.

This report was approved by the Committee on Fiscal Affairs on 4 June 2021 and prepared for publication by the OECD Secretariat.

Table of contents

FIGURES

TABLES

Follow OECD Publications on:

http://twitter.com/OECD_Pubs

http://www.facebook.com/OECDPublications

http://www.linkedin.com/groups/OECD-Publications-4645871

http://www.youtube.com/oecdilibrary

http://www.oecd.org/oecddirect/

Abbreviations and Acronyms

AML	Anti-money laundering
EOI	Exchange of information
FATF	Financial Action Task Force
FIU	Financial Intelligence Unit
GST	Goods and Services Tax
MLAT	Mutual Legal Assistance Treaty
OECD	Organisation for Economic Co-operation and Development
STR	Suspicious Transaction Report
TFTC	Task Force on Tax Crimes and Other Crimes
TIEA	Tax Information Exchange Agreement
UNODC	United Nations Office on Drugs and Crime
VAT	Value Added Tax

Executive Summary

As the world emerges from the COVID-19 pandemic, tax and other financial crimes are more global than ever which, if unchecked, can undermine the rule of law as well as public confidence in the legal and financial system. Technological developments are also leading to the emergence of new risks including through the growth of cybercrimes, the increasing misuse of cryptocurrencies and a new breed of sophisticated professional enablers able to create opaque structures and move money increasingly in real-time.

As the world recovers from the effects of the pandemic, fighting tax crimes takes on a new imperative. This calls for increasing international co-operation and for all jurisdictions to have a robust domestic set of legal and operational tools in place to effectively detect, disrupt and sanction tax crime offenders and the enablers of tax crime.

In support of these objectives, this guide updates the first edition of the Ten Global Principles for Fighting Tax Crimes, which has been highly influential in providing an internationally recognised framework against which countries can benchmark themselves and take inspiration. The Ten Global Principles cover the full range of tools that countries should strive for, from having comprehensive laws in place that criminalise tax offences, to the establishment of an overarching tax crime strategy for detecting threats and targeting criminal activity, as well as having the mechanisms in place to confiscate the proceeds of the offence after a conviction.

This new edition of the Ten Global Principles provides an update on their implementation around the globe, with 33 country chapters setting out both the progress that has been made as well as recommendations for further improvements. The report also highlights the value of tax crime investigation agencies, both in monetary terms and in the impact they have on the disruption of crime and on maintaining public confidence. While this report calls for granting tax crime agencies a wide range of investigative and enforcement powers, it also stresses the importance of suspects' rights in the course of an investigation, including the presumption of innocence, the right to a lawyer, and access to full disclosure of incriminatory evidence.

Drawing from the first edition, published in 2017, from further work by the OECD Task Force on Tax Crimes and Other Crimes (TFTC), and from inputs received by 33 jurisdictions, the second edition of the Ten Global Principles shows that, overall, jurisdictions continue to enhance their abilities to tackle tax crime, both domestically and internationally. All surveyed jurisdictions have comprehensive laws in place that criminalise tax offences, and the ability to apply strong penalties, including lengthy prison sentences, substantial fines, asset forfeiture and a range of alternative sanctions. Jurisdictions generally have a wide range of investigative and enforcement powers in place as well as access to relevant data and intelligence. Nearly all participating jurisdictions consider tax crimes as predicate offences for money laundering. Suspects' rights are nearly universally understood in the same way and enshrined in law.

However, as noted above, tax crimes are changing as criminals employ new technology tools and cross-border offences are becoming more widespread. The second edition of this report underlines that jurisdictions need to engage actively in cross-border co-operation in the fight against tax crimes, including through the use of information-sharing mechanisms, and by incorporating counter-strategies against professional enablers into their national strategies. As cases become more complex, setting up joint taskforces and intelligence-sharing groups, both in the domestic and international arena, becomes increasingly important.

Recommendations

This new edition of the 10 Global Principles guide recommends that jurisdictions benchmark themselves against each of the Principles. This includes identifying areas where changes in law or operational aspects are needed, such as increasing the type of investigative or enforcement powers, expanding access to other government-held data, developing or updating the strategy for addressing tax offences, and taking greater efforts to measure impacts.

It also recommends that jurisdictions that have committed to support capacity building for developing jurisdictions in tax matters, including through the Addis Tax Initiative or the G7 Bari Declaration, consider how they can best work with developing jurisdictions to enhance tax crime investigation and promote the wider adoption of the Ten Principles. Options include providing expert trainers for the OECD International Academy for Tax and Financial Crime Investigation, joining the pilot Tax Inspectors without Borders programme for Criminal Investigations, supporting the roll-out of the Tax Crime Investigation Maturity Model and through other regional or bilateral initiatives.

The Task Force on Tax Crimes and Other Crimes (TFTC) will continue its work in facilitating international co-operation on fighting tax crime, particularly on issues where multilateral action is required to address common challenges, such as asset recovery and tackling professional enablers.

This could also include collaborating to create an agreed strategy for addressing tax crimes that have cross-border elements. Drawing from the experience of existing initiatives, such a strategy could include mechanisms for cooperation on identifying risks, including potentially widening available data sources, and for ensuring that data and information sharing agreements are available and work well in practice.

Overview of the Ten Global Principles

This guide is part of the OECD's ongoing work on the Oslo Dialogue, a whole of government approach to fighting tax crimes and other financial crimes. The second edition of the Ten Global Principles draws from countries' experience in applying the first edition of the report, published in 2017, from the work conducted by the OECD Task Force on Tax Crimes and Other Crimes (TFTC) since then, and from specific inputs received from more than 30 jurisdictions across the world.

The second edition of this report analyses successful case studies and best practices, as described by participating jurisdictions, while defining emerging trends in the field of tax crimes in particular, and financial crimes in general. It also draws on the recent OECD publications on the Tax Crime Investigation Maturity Model (OECD, 2020[1]) and "Ending the Shell Game: Cracking Down on the Professionals who enable Tax and White Collar Crimes" (OECD, 2021[2]).

Drawing on the knowledge and experience of government agencies around the world, this guide sets out Ten Global Principles for effectively fighting tax crime. Each Principle is described, and supplemented with examples and current practices from around the world.

This guide is intended to serve three purposes:

1. Allowing jurisdictions to benchmark their legal and operational framework to identify successful practices to improve their processes and systems for fighting tax crimes;
2. Allowing the measurement and tracking of the progress of jurisdictions through regular updates
3. Allowing jurisdictions to articulate their needs for training for both developing and developed jurisdictions, including by incorporating the guide into the OECD International Academy for Tax and Financial Crime Investigation[1] curriculum.

Naturally, jurisdictions' implementation of the Ten Global Principles reflects the broader context of their legal system, administrative practice and culture. It is up to each jurisdiction to decide how best to implement the Ten Global Principles in a manner that is most appropriate in the context of, and most consistent with, its legal framework, the organisational structure for fighting tax crimes and compliance with the jurisdiction's commitments and obligations under international standards, conventions and, in the case of European Union member states, European Union law.

In addition, each jurisdiction has a different definition of tax crime, and a different organisational structure for investigating tax crime and other financial crimes. As such, in this report, references to "tax crime" are intended to mean intentional conduct that violates a tax law and can be investigated, prosecuted and sentenced under criminal procedures within the criminal justice system. This definition is intended to be broad enough to accommodate the different legal definitions that may apply under domestic law. It is intended to cover the violation of both income tax law obligations, as well as indirect tax obligations (such as VAT or GST). This report does not include other financial crimes such as the violation of customs and excise taxes, corruption, bribery or money-laundering laws, although of course will be of relevance in those areas as well.

This guide presents a picture of current practices in order to help jurisdictions to review and evaluate their own implementation of the Ten Global Principles, especially in comparison to relevant peers. This guide includes tables and charts reflecting statistical and other data supplied by 33 jurisdictions in response to a survey conducted through 2019 to early 2021. However, comparisons should be made with considerable care in the absence of uniform law and practices across jurisdictions. In particular, the statistics compiled cannot adjust for variations in terminology (legal terms and definitions), tax and legal systems; the size and population of jurisdictions and size of respective tax administrations; different approaches to tax risk and overall rates of compliance; and other compliance approaches / strategies applied (such as any preference for civil penalties over criminal prosecutions in particular circumstances). As such, the statistics in this guide should not be considered in isolation, but in the context of a jurisdiction's broader approach to tax compliance and fighting financial crimes.

This guide is accompanied of individual country chapters in which jurisdictions have benchmarked themselves against the Ten Global Principles. While the intention is that this report will stay as an open document, available for any jurisdiction willing to participate in the benchmarking exercise in the future, the statistics and successful case studies in this edition were last updated in April 2021, and comprise data from Argentina, Australia, Austria, Azerbaijan, Brazil, Canada, Chile, Colombia, Costa Rica, Czech Republic, Estonia, France, Georgia, Germany, Greece, Honduras, Hungary, Iceland, Ireland, Israel, Italy, Japan, Korea, Mexico, Netherlands, New Zealand, Norway, South Africa, Spain, Sweden, Switzerland, the United Kingdom and the United States.

References

OECD (2021), Ending the Shell Game: Cracking down on the Professionals who enable Tax and White Collar Crimes, OECD, https://www.oecd.org/tax/crime/ending-the-shell-game-cracking-down-on-the-professionals-who-enable-tax-and-white-collar-crimes.htm.

OECD (2020), Tax Crime Investigation Maturity Model, OECD, https://www.oecd.org/tax/crime/tax-crime-investigation-maturity-model.htm.

Note

[1] OECD International Academy for Tax and Financial Crime Investigation, available at: https://www.oecd.org/tax/crime/tax-crime-academy.

Principle 1 Ensure tax offences are criminalised

Jurisdictions should have the legal framework in place to ensure that violations of tax law are included as a criminal offence, and that effective sanctions apply in practice.

Introduction

1.   Most taxpayers voluntarily comply with their tax obligations. However, some taxpayers persevere in being non-compliant and use any means to evade their tax obligations. It is in respect of those taxpayers, for whom support and monitoring does not improve compliance, that criminal law plays an important role. Moreover, it enhances the general preventive effect that criminal law enforcement can have and reduces non-compliance.

2.   Jurisdictions draw different conclusions as to precisely when the application of the criminal law is warranted. The provisions of the criminal law define the actions that are designated as tax crimes as well as the type of criminal sanctions that are considered appropriate. These defined actions and criminal sanctions will not be the same in all jurisdictions.

3.   Wherever dividing lines between non-compliant behaviour and criminal behaviour are drawn, it is important that jurisdictions have the possibility of applying criminal sanctions in respect of violations of the tax law. From a preventive point of view, this is for several reasons:

  i.   to send a message about the integrity, neutrality and fairness of the law (that is, that nobody is above the law)

  ii.   to act as a general deterrent for those people that could be tempted to evade their tax obligations if the opportunity arose, by providing serious reputational and punitive consequences of such activity;

iii. to act as a specific deterrent for an individual that has been convicted and sanctioned in the past, so that they might be discouraged from doing so again. Actual enforcement of penal provisions for the purposes of punishment for those that have decided not to comply is essential for both doing justice and strengthening the credibility of the penal provisions and the legal system itself.

4.   The criminalisation of violations of tax law also ensures the availability of criminal investigative and enforcement powers that are necessary to find the truth regardless of the co-operation of the accused. In some jurisdictions this also provides for a basis for domestic co-operation with other law enforcement agencies under criminal law and international co-operation, for example, under an MLAT.

5.   The precise way of criminalising violations of tax law will vary from one jurisdiction to another. Each jurisdiction has a different legal system, which reflects and interacts with the particular culture, policy and legislative environment.

6.   Whatever the particular details of the legal framework are, it will be most effective if:

- The law clearly defines the tax offences that are criminalised;
- A criminal sanction applies if the offence is proven;
- More serious offences are punishable by more serious criminal sanctions; and
- Criminal sanctions are applied in practice.

The law clearly defines the tax offences that are criminalised

7.   The offences within the tax crime category may be defined in a general manner to capture a wide range of activities such as criminal actions that intend to defraud the government. A different approach is where the law sets out the specific offences in more detail, each with individual requirements as to the precise actions that constitute a crime.

8.   Whichever definitional approach is taken, jurisdictions may also take different approaches to the threshold at which an act is classified as an offence. For instance, jurisdictions may criminalise actions starting from non-compliance, such as any deliberate failure to correctly file a tax return. Some other jurisdictions may apply the criminal law starting from a higher threshold, where the deliberate failure to comply with a tax obligation is accompanied by aggravating factors such as if the amount of tax evaded exceeds a certain monetary threshold, if the offence is committed repeatedly, when taxable income is actively concealed, or when records or evidence are deliberately falsified. Alternatively, jurisdictions may have set a very high threshold to classify tax crime, such as organised crime for profit, or tax evasion accompanied by particularly aggravating circumstances. Common examples are included below:

Category	Examples
Non-compliance offences (may apply irrespective of intent or result)	• Failure to provide required information, documents or returns • Failure to register for tax purposes • Failure to keep records • Keeping incorrect records • Making a false statement • Non-payment
Intentional tax offences	• Destroying records • Deliberate failure to comply with tax law to obtain financial advantage • Evading tax or receiving refunds by fraud or illegal practices • Intentional reduction of tax using false documents or fictitious invoices • Counterfeit or forged documents to reduce tax • Intentionally or by gross negligence providing misleading information in a tax return to obtain a tax advantage

	• Fraudulently obtaining refunds or credit
	• Tax evasion in aggravated circumstances such as cases involving considerable financial benefit or conducted in a methodical manner
	• Theft from, or defrauding of the government
	• Obstructing an official of the tax authority
	• Accessory offences
Specific offences	• Entering an arrangement that would make person unable to pay tax
	• Committing tax evasion as member of an organised criminal group
	• Commercial commission of tax evasion
	• Illegal use of "zappers" or other automated sale suppression software or devices
	• Identity theft

9.   Jurisdictions should also criminalise the act of aiding, abetting, facilitating or enabling the commission of a tax offence by others, or conspiracy to commit a tax offence, ("accessories"), such as actions taken by professional enablers (see below).

10.   Jurisdictions may, for example, include these criminal offences within a statute or code covering all criminal activities, in a general tax act, in their income tax or VAT statutes, or other specific statutes. Whichever approaches are used, the legal provisions should state the elements that constitute the crime. This includes articulating the specific conduct or activity that constitutes the criminal act, as well as the required mental state of the person in committing the activity (such as intention, recklessness or gross negligence). These offences should be laid down in statutes by using clear terms, which would prevent potential disagreements and misunderstandings regarding terminology by both taxpayers and the criminal justice system.

11.   In addition to prosecuting individuals, jurisdictions should be able to prosecute legal persons and legal arrangements for committing a tax crime. For example, where tax evasion has been conducted by a company, there may not be an identifiable individual responsible for the crime, but the criminal actions may have occurred because of the combined actions of several persons undertaken in their capacity as representatives of the company. The law may hold the legal person or arrangement criminally liable for the crime, and also impose punishment on key actors such as directors, officers, agents or key employees of the legal person / arrangement criminally liable. The ability to hold entities criminally responsible amongst survey respondents is as follows:

Figure 1.1. The ability to hold entities criminally responsible

Is it possible to hold legal entities criminally liable for criminal tax offences?

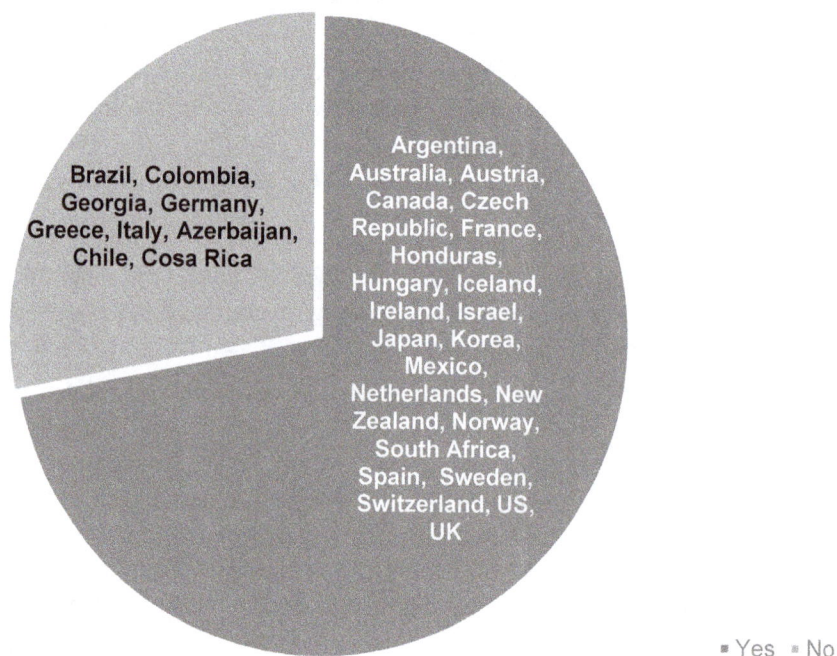

Brazil, Colombia, Georgia, Germany, Greece, Italy, Azerbaijan, Chile, Cosa Rica

Argentina, Australia, Austria, Canada, Czech Republic, France, Honduras, Hungary, Iceland, Ireland, Israel, Japan, Korea, Mexico, Netherlands, New Zealand, Norway, South Africa, Spain, Sweden, Switzerland, US, UK

▪ Yes ▪ No

A criminal sanction applies if the offence is proven

12.   The legal provision should include a penalty if the elements of the crime are proven. Penalties should be designed to encourage compliance and prevent non-compliance by providing a credible threat. Any statute of limitations on imposing a criminal penalty should reflect the seriousness of the crime and the prescribed punishment. A practical consequence of having a sufficiently long statute of limitations for serious crimes is that it provides agencies with sufficient time to identify and prosecute criminal acts. This is especially important in respect of complex cases which can take a long time to successfully investigate and prosecute.

Figure 1.2. Maximum prison sentence for a tax offence (years) – income tax and VAT

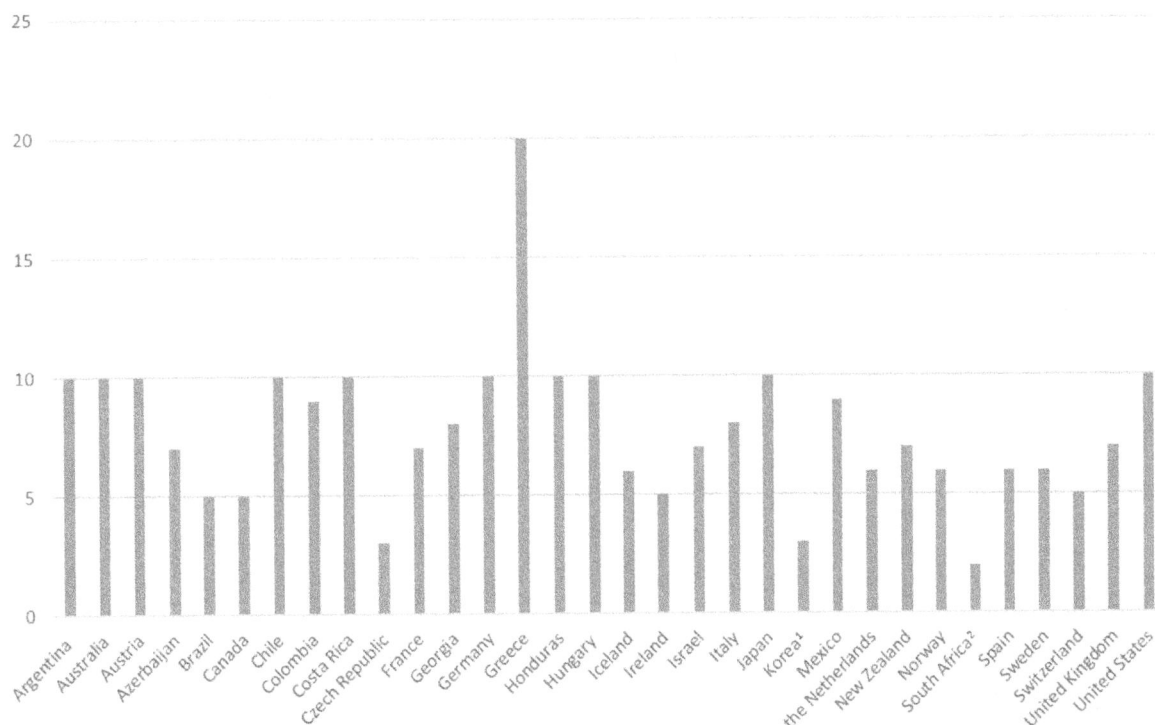

1. Korean law provides that cases of aggravated tax evasion, where the amount of evaded tax is over KRW 500 million in a year, can be sentenced to imprisonment for an indefinite term.
2. South Africa notes that it is able to secure significantly longer sentences where there are multiple offences and the sum of the sentences run consecutively or, where it is successful, under the common law offence of fraud.

More serious offences are punishable by more serious criminal sanctions

13.   There is a range of behaviour that can constitute a tax crime. In order to achieve the objectives of criminalising tax offences stated above, more serious behaviour or crimes committed in graver circumstances should be punishable by more serious criminal sanctions, proportionate to the nature of the offence.

14.   As discussed above, each jurisdiction will have its own approach to categorising the types of offences and their seriousness. Whatever the approach is, the seriousness of the offence should be reflected in the seriousness of the consequences for the offender.

A penalty regime is in place for prosecuting professional enablers

15.   Even though the majority of professionals are law-abiding and play an important role in assisting businesses and individuals to understand and comply with the law, jurisdictions should have a penalty regime in place to tackle the small sub-set of professionals who use their skills and knowledge to facilitate the commission of tax and other financial crimes by their clients. Such professionals, which may include lawyers, accountants and tax advisors, play an integral role in making it easier for taxpayers to defraud the government and evade tax obligations, including by designing non-transparent structures and schemes to conceal the true identity of the individuals behind the illegal activities undertaken.

16.   Governments have increasingly recognised the need to actively pursue these professional enablers. Several jurisdictions responded that accessories, including professional enablers, are criminally responsible, and in most cases can be held liable for the same offence and the same criminal sanction. In some cases, the person can be liable for an increased penalty, such as where they are a tax professional and their facilitation of the offence is considered to be an aggravating factor. There are also jurisdictions which also apply significant civil penalties for professional enablers or promoters. A breakdown of this, based on survey data, is shown below:

Table 1.1. Types of regimes in places for prosecuting professional enablers

May be prosecuted under general rules for primary or secondary offenders	Special penalty regime in place	Non-criminal sanction
Austria	Argentina[1]	Australia
Azerbaijan	Chile[2]	France[3]
Brazil	Israel	Netherlands[4]
Canada	Italy	Ireland[5]
Colombia	Korea	
Costa Rica	Mexico	
Czech Republic[6]	Sweden	
France	United Kingdom	
Georgia	United States	
Germany		
Greece		
Honduras		
Hungary		
Japan		
Netherlands		
New Zealand		
Norway		
South Africa		
Spain		
Switzerland		

1. Special sanction for professional enablers on the Tax Crimes Law.
2. Special offence in the Tax Code.
3. France may apply both the general rules of primary/secondary criminal participation and an administrative sanction.
4. The Netherlands may apply both the general rules of primary/secondary criminal participation and an administrative sanction.
5. Sanctions, including disqualification, may be applied by the professional governing bodies.
6. May be considered an aggravating circumstance.

Criminal sanctions are applied in practice

17.   The law that criminalises tax offences should be enforced. Where the offence is proven in a court proceeding, the criminal sanction that is most likely to be effective and is appropriate to the facts and circumstances should be applied. Penalties should be applied fairly and consistently.

18.   Depending on the case, imposing a monetary penalty may be appropriate. For example, in respect of surveyed jurisdictions where data was available, fines were imposed by the competent authorities in respect of violations of the tax law for over EUR 1.4 billion in 2017.

19.   It may be appropriate for alternative types of criminal sanctions to apply, depending on the relevant case. These can include community service, "naming and shaming" offenders or enablers, disqualification

from holding certain offices, suspension of licence or other privileges, specific orders to forfeit or return assets, or a combination of the above.

20.   9 of the 31 surveyed jurisdictions responded that they have used sanctions other than imprisonment or a fine between 2015 and 2018.[1]

Figure 1.3. Alternative sanctions imposed between 2015 and 2018 in respect of tax offences

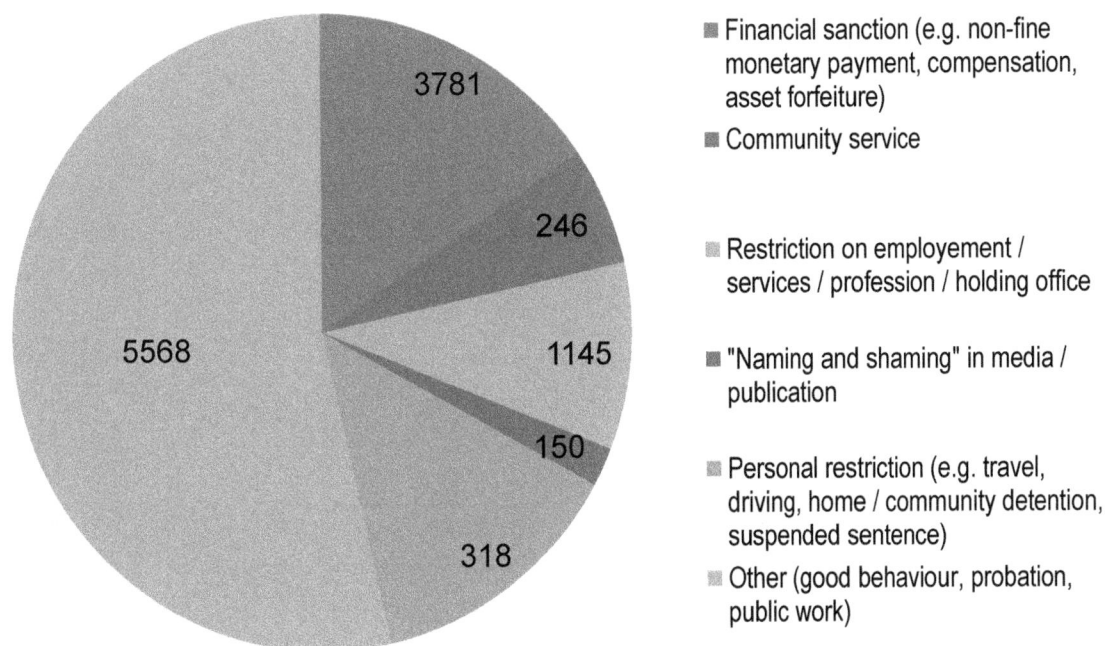

- Financial sanction (e.g. non-fine monetary payment, compensation, asset forfeiture)
- Community service
- Restriction on employement / services / profession / holding office
- "Naming and shaming" in media / publication
- Personal restriction (e.g. travel, driving, home / community detention, suspended sentence)
- Other (good behaviour, probation, public work)

References

OECD (2021), *Ending the Shell Game: Cracking down on the Professionals who enable Tax and White Collar Crimes*, OECD, https://www.oecd.org/tax/crime/ending-the-shell-game-cracking-down-on-the-professionals-who-enable-tax-and-white-collar-crimes.htm.

Note

[1] Australia, Azerbaijan, Canada, Czech Republic, France, Georgia, Mexico, New Zealand, United States.

Principle 2 Devise an effective strategy for addressing tax crimes

In order to ensure the effectiveness of the law on tax crimes, jurisdictions should have a strategy for addressing tax crimes. The strategy should be regularly reviewed and monitored.

Introduction

21. To be most effective in addressing tax crimes, tax authorities need to have a range of strategies for encouraging compliance, to effectively respond to the different attitudes of taxpayers to complying with their obligations. To ensure that the laws related to tax crimes are effective in practice, a coherent strategy for enforcing the law should be devised. An overall strategy can be described as a document which states the objective of the tax authorities, identifies the relevant risks of non-compliance with the tax law, and sets out the plan for addressing those risks. There should be buy-in from senior officials who are accountable for delivering the overall strategy.

22. Generally, there should be an overall tax compliance strategy that covers the full range of compliance, from encouraging voluntary compliance, dealing with inadvertent non-compliance, to avoidance, evasion and serious crime. However, the specific strategy would be based on each jurisdiction's legal system, policy context, legislative environment and general structure of law enforcement. The figure below sets out examples of measures that can be taken to enhance compliance.

Tax fraud (serious organised crime)	Combatting and preventing fraud	Anti-fraud measures	• Tax investigation and audits • Prosecution and penalties • Elimination from legal financial circles • Cooperation with the judicial system/police
Tax evasion (shadow economy, income underreporting, illegal employment)	Controls and sanctions		• Controls, investigations • Tax audits (risk analysis) • Prosecution and penalties • Tax collection
Tax avoidance (aggressive tax planning, avoidance models)	Monitoring and cooperation		• Risk management • Office and field staff controls • Official first visits • Tax collection
Tax compliance (voluntary disclosure, fulfilment of tax obligations)	Support and simplification		• Information and forms • Cooperation with interest groups • Horizontal monitoring • Advance rulings

Identifying the risks and threats

23.   A strategy may be most effective if a threat assessment is first undertaken, because knowing the relevant threats will ensure the response can be targeted to address those threats. All tax authorities have a finite level of resources, which must be allocated efficiently on the basis of priorities. To do this, the tax authority should have a process for identifying the threats that are posed to the enforcement of the tax laws, and how serious these are. Ideally a threat assessment will include current, emerging and future risks.

24.   The benefit of conducting regular threat assessments is that it provides a structured basis for actively considering the current, emerging and future risks. Such a process supports improved decision-making by informed priority setting on how to address the various degrees of non-compliance, including combatting tax crimes, more effectively.

25.   A threat assessment identifies the specific risks of tax crimes that are prevalent in the jurisdiction. This should take into account the particular context or environment (cultural, political, legal, economic and technological), and where relevant, draw on the insights of other agencies responsible for fighting financial crimes. It can be effective to prioritise the threats in terms of the likelihood and the impact if such threats are realised.

26.   A number of surveyed jurisdictions take steps to identify and assess the threats on an ongoing basis. This often takes the form of regular environmental scans, intelligence and trend / forecast analysis. A wide range of intelligence sources tend to be taken into account to identify emerging threats, such as all available information from the tax authority, observations of investigators and feedback from completed cases, asset databases, currency transaction data, open source intelligence, and intelligence from other agencies such as police, social services, prosecution, corruption, procurement, labour agencies, customs, immigration or border authorities, as well as from the private sector and from members of the public. Several jurisdictions reported that the analysis of the threats considers the possible revenue impact, frequency of the threat, likelihood of threat materialising and coherence with other strategic priorities.

27.   The results of the threat assessment may assist in identifying specific needs, such as to establish a cross-agency task force to address a particular risk, to launch a public awareness campaign, to build technical capacity in a particular area, to engage with the private sector or to inform the need for changes in the law.

Key elements of an overall strategy

28.   There are many different ways of designing an overall strategy. The following diagram illustrates a possible approach to preparing a strategy, including the need for the results to feedback into the revision of the strategy.

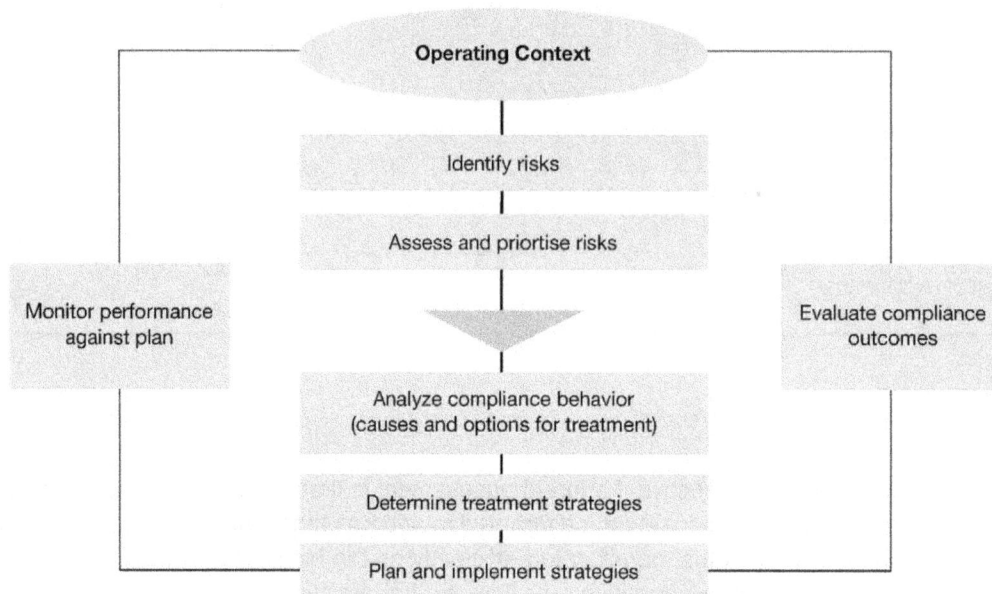

Source: Russell, B (2010), *Revenue Administration: Developing a Taxpayer Compliance Program*, International Monetary Fund, The United States of America.

29.   Taking account of the threat assessment, an effective strategy can be prepared which may include the following elements:

- Defining the objectives / performance indicators / outputs. For example, this could be organised around the goals of prevention, detection and enforcement.

- Articulating the resources available to address these risks (including legal powers, funding, personnel, expertise, stakeholders in other government agencies, sources of intelligence, investigation and enforcement tools including domestic and international co-operation).

- Identifying the challenges for the tax authority in being able to address the risks and how those challenges can be mitigated.

- Devising an operational plan for achieving the objectives for the identified risks, using the available resources and tools and including criminal law enforcement.

- Preparing a communications strategy. This is important in order to shape public perceptions and behaviour, as it can be a reminder of the serious criminal sanctions that can be imposed and act as a deterrent when high profile cases are prosecuted. It can also help to educate the public, and build public confidence in the fair enforcement of tax laws.

- A plan for periodically reviewing performance and measuring the effectiveness and currency of the compliance strategy.

30.   It is important that the strategy is based on wide consultation with all relevant stakeholders such as policy makers, investigators, enforcement and prosecution officials and other agencies such as AML authorities, in accordance with each jurisdiction's legal system, policy and legislative environment and general structure of law enforcement. In particular, given that serious tax crimes are likely to raise other matters of criminal law such as money laundering (especially as tax crimes are in most cases a predicate offence for money laundering, as set out in Principle 7 below), jurisdictions should consider including tax crimes in an overall serious crime strategy, or a strategy specifically for addressing financial crimes. A number of jurisdictions prepare their strategies in co-ordination with other agencies, such as anti-corruption, economic crime units, police, the prosecutor, financial intelligence unit, customs, securities regulators and the ministry of justice. For example:

- Norway has a national strategy for tackling the shadow labour market and economic crime.
- Austria has both a specific Tax and Customs Compliance strategy as well as annual Internal Security Strategy which focus more broadly on economic crime and money laundering.
- The United Kingdom's tax authority contributes to the National Strategic Assessment for Serious and Organised Crime.

31.   It is also important that the strategy for addressing tax crimes includes a mechanism for criminal and non-criminal tax officials to share expertise, processes and intelligence. This is because the officials responsible for non-criminal tax matters and for criminal matters will often have a symbiotic relationship; for example, the non-criminal function will have relevant intelligence for investigating tax crimes, both on specific cases as well as general trends. Likewise, the criminal function will also have information relevant for civil tax compliance, including on cases where it was not possible to pursue a criminal conviction but where a civil audit may be appropriate, or where information about a criminal conviction may be useful in taking forward a civil process.

32.   Strategic co-ordination between the criminal and non-criminal tax officials can help to ensure a coherent use of resources, efficient prioritisation of cases and avoid duplication of efforts by both the tax administration and criminal law enforcement officials. It should also increase taxpayer compliance overall, provide a deterrent effect when the public is aware of the effective co-operation between the criminal and non-criminal functions, and enhance the perceived fairness for the compliant taxpayer. This co-ordination will have to also take into account mechanisms for protecting the rights of a person if and when a matter has criminal aspects (see Principles 6 and 10 for further information).

33.   All surveyed jurisdictions had a process for civil tax officials to refer suspicions of tax crimes to the relevant law enforcement authority, and in most cases there was a legal obligation to do so. Key features which ensured the effectiveness of this process included training for civil tax officials to be able to identify indicators of a crime; having a clearly identified and central contact point for sending referrals; using a standard form that ensured all relevant data was captured for use by the criminal investigation authority; and meetings for feedback between the civil and criminal investigators including during the process for deciding how to proceed with the individual referrals.

34.   The exact steps for referrals will depend on each jurisdiction's legal and operational framework. For instance, civil tax auditors in jurisdictions such as Argentina and in Brazil have a legal obligation to report any suspicion of crime, including tax crime, to the competent law enforcement agencies.

35.   In France, suspicions of tax crime leading to tax recalls of over EUR 100 000 are directly referred to the public prosecution service. Cases of less than EUR 100 000 are submitted to the *Commission des Infractions Fiscales* (CIF), an independent administrative authority mandated to analyse the referral before directing it to the prosecution service. France notes that it had compulsorily referred 965 civil tax audits for

criminal investigation in 2019, and that the CIF had allowed the commencement of further 672 criminal investigations for tax fraud of less than EUR 100 000 in the same period.

36.   Referrals of suspicions of tax crime are taken into account in the Key Performance Indicators of Canada's revenue agency.

Jurisdiction examples of strategies for addressing tax crimes

37.   The United Kingdom has a range of documents that contribute to its overall strategy for the prevention, investigation, and prosecution of tax crimes. In March 2019, Her Majesty's Revenue and Customs (HMRC), in partnership with Her Majesty's Treasury (HMT) published the United Kingdom's approach to tackling tax avoidance, evasion, and other forms of noncompliance. (HMRC & HMT, 2019[1]) This document outlines the United Kingdom's strategy and approach to compliance for different taxpayers. As part of its overall strategy, the United Kingdom conducts intensive threat assessments, and HMRC consults with a variety of stakeholders including law enforcement agencies, other government departments, international partners and the private sector.

38.   The Netherlands' Fiscal Intelligence and Investigation Service (FIOD), works in close co-operation with the wider Tax and Customs Administration (NTCA), and Public Prosecution Service (OM) on what it describes as a 'combined enforcement practice'. The strategy calls for fast and flexible decision-making process supported by guidelines and protocols. For example, the 'Protocol for the Notification and Settlement of Fiscal Offences and Offences Relating to Customs and Allowances' describes how the NTCA, FIOD, and OM make a joint decision on whether or not to open a criminal investigation into tax and customs offences. The protocol sets out criteria for when a matter becomes eligible for possible criminal proceedings (based on intentional acts, amounts involved etc.). In addition, the three bodies also agree on an 'Enforcement Strategy Arrangement' on an annual basis, which sets out a plan for dealing with violations of tax, financial, and economical laws and regulations including co-operation agreements between enforcement partners, the deployment of interventions, the impact of prosecution on society, and future developments. The use of media, digitalisation, innovation, and the prioritising of relevant themes are all taken into account in this strategy.

39.   Israel's tax crime strategy seeks to deepen the co-operation between the Israeli Police, the Israeli Tax Authority (ITA), the Securities Authority, the Ministry of Justice, the Antitrust Authority, and the AML authority. The result of the strategy is a new combined enforcement structure, which enhances the ability of these agencies to conduct joint enforcement operations. Israel notes that the new enforcement structure resulted in a number of investigations that would otherwise not have been possible, whereby each agency contributes its own expertise. Furthermore, ITA conducts meetings with law and tax professionals (from associations such as the Israel Bar, the Accountants Council and tax consultants), in order to promote better enforcement of tax legislation.

Box 2.1. Risk assessment exercises for detecting involvement of professional enablers

Many jurisdictions have dedicated teams focused on compliance work specifically relating to a known problem area, such as targeting enablers that are associated with multiple shell companies or that market the use of offshore structures. For example, jurisdictions have collected information on professional enablers connected to offshore service providers or firms for the purpose of utilising it in data analytics and audit strategies. Feedback from jurisidctions shows that offshore jurisdictions known as "hotspots" of activity for specific evasion structures are often utilised repeatedly by the same professional enablers. Once a particular structure or nefarious service provider is uncovered, this gives tax authorities the ability to target other structures established by the same professional enablers. However, feedback also shows that these hotspots can fluctuate, for example in response to detection or where a new strategy is devised, and therefore national professional enabler strategies need to be flexible to adapt to new information and intelligence received.

For risk assessment exercises to include an analysis involvement of professional enablers, some of the following indicators could be deployed:

- A company is not found at the declared premises
- Addresses of entities or directors which are not traceable
- Multiple shell companies from the same address
- Multiple companies with directors in common
- Company's address registered at a P.O. Box address known for illegitimate businesses
- Professionals with a high turnover of business relating to liquidation of small companies
- Professionals that promote tax schemes on the basis of premium or contingent fees, orcontractual protection that guarantees coverage of any financial liabilities resulting from the tax strategy
- Where one individual is attributed as a director multiple times, the extent to which the provision of substantial and meaningful directorship services could not be feasible
- Tax intermediaries with poor tax compliance and filing history • Persons with association to known professional enablers
- Persons with association to known tax evasion structures
- Persons with association to known offshore structures that obscure beneficial ownership to facilitate fraudulent behaviour

Source: OECD (2021), Ending the Shell Game: Cracking down on the Professionals who enable Tax and White Collar Crimes, OECD Publishing, Paris.

References

HMRC & HMT (2019), *Tackling tax avoidance, evasion, and other forms of non-compliance*, https://assets.publishing.service.gov.uk/government/uploads/system/uploads/attachment _data/file/785551/tackling_tax_avoidance_evasion_and_other_forms_of_non-compliance_web.pdf.   [1]

Principle 3 Have adequate investigative powers

Jurisdictions must have appropriate investigative powers to successfully investigate tax crimes.

Introduction

40.   The standard purpose of a criminal (tax) investigation is to find the truth by investigating the alleged criminal (tax) behaviour. In conducting an investigation, criminal investigators will generally seek to find and analyse information for the purposes of determining whether or not a crime has been committed. Investigations can result in finding both incriminating ("inculpatory") evidence and evidence that confirms innocence ("exculpatory evidence"). This is used for prosecution authorities to decide whether or not to prosecute the accused. As criminals seek to hide the criminal nature of their conduct, criminal law enforcement agencies need an appropriate range of investigative powers in order to obtain the necessary information. In particular, in the context of investigating tax offences, there is significant value in being able to effectively investigate the source and movement of financial assets. This can be essential to establish the commission of fraud, and to identify the role of an intermediary or accessory, even where the assets themselves have been moved.

41.   Depending on which agency has responsibility for investigating tax crimes (see Principle 5 for more details), the nature and extent of investigatory powers in a particular agency may vary. In general, the competency for conducting criminal tax investigations will fall within one of these four models, as described in the Effective Inter-agency Co-operation In Fighting Tax Crimes And Other Financial Crimes, Third Edition, 2017 (the "Rome Report") (OECD, 2017[1]).

General Organisational Models for Investigating Tax Crimes			
Model 1	**Model 2**	**Model 3**	**Model 4**
Tax administration directs and conducts investigations	Tax administration conducts investigations, directed by prosecutor	Specialist agency outside tax administration conducts tax offence investigations, which may involve public prosecutors	Police or public prosecutor conduct investigations

42.   A tax administration conducting criminal tax investigations under organisational Model 1 may not always have the full range of investigative powers, expertise or resources, such as the ability to search and seize, intercept communications and demand production of documents. If the tax administration is responsible for conducting criminal tax investigations but does not have the full range of investigative powers itself, these powers should still be available indirectly where needed, such as through the ability to call on the police or another agency to provide investigatory services.

43.   Under organisational Model 2 and under Model 4, where the police or public prosecutor conducts and/or directs the investigations, the investigative powers will most likely be similar to the investigative powers of the police conducting other financial investigations. Under Model 3, an agency separate to the tax administration is responsible for investigating tax crime cases, and the investigative powers are also likely to be similar to the investigative powers of the police.

44.   Whichever organisational model is used, the agencies responsible for investigating tax offences should have the investigative powers that it considers are necessary and effective in the context of its own mandate, and taking into account the ability to work with other law enforcement agencies which may have additional powers. These investigative powers should allow accessing information and evidence in the digital world in addition to the more traditional sources of information.

45.   The availability of relevant investigative powers amongst survey respondents is set out below. Throughout this section of the guide, it is noted that the precise circumstances and legal procedures that need to be followed in order to use such powers vary. The representation of jurisdictions as having "direct powers" is not intended to reflect that the power can be used in all investigations of a tax offence, but that the agency is able to exercise the powers itself in the authorised circumstances (including circumstances where a warrant or court authorisation is granted to the agency). The reference to having indirect powers via another agency reflects an arrangement where the power would be exercised by a different agency outside the criminal tax investigation agency, such as by the police.

Powers to obtain third party documentary information

46.   The power to obtain information may be needed to access documents and information from financial institutions and other third parties. These powers require a third party to hand over documents or information within a specified amount of time. If the demand is not met, more intrusive powers that involve a physical search of property or digital media may follow. The power to obtain third party documentary information is particularly appropriate where the information sought is not readily available in a physical form (e.g. banks which do not maintain paper copies of a customer's bank statements or telecommunications providers' data) since this power allows the third party time to collect the demanded material. These powers can take the form of a subpoena, production order, or other powers to demand or compel the handing over of documentary information. This power is available in survey respondents as follows:

Table 3.1. Powers to obtain third party documentary information

Full direct powers Agency responsible for tax crime investigation can be authorised to exercise the power itself			Indirect powers via another agency Agency responsible for tax crime investigation can seek assistance of another agency to exercise the power on its behalf	Not available
Argentina	Germany[5]	The Netherlands	Australia[11]	
Australia[1]	Greece[6]	New Zealand	Brazil	
Austria	Honduras	Norway	Sweden[12]	
Azerbaijan	Hungary	South Africa		
Canada	Iceland	Spain[8]		
Chile	Ireland	Sweden[9]		
Colombia	Israel	Switzerland[10]		
Costa Rica[2]	Italy	United States		
Czech Republic[3]	Japan	United Kingdom		
France	Korea			
Georgia[4]	Mexico[7]			

1. AFP.
2. Civil investigators have the power to obtain documents for third parties without a warrant (except in the case of financial information, in which case it requires judicial authorization). The Prosecutor's Office can also use this power, but only after obtaining a warrant from a judge.
3. Police.
4. Investigators must submit a written request to the court, which then decides whether or not to grant a warrant to obtain third party documents.
5. A court order is generally required. An exception applies in cases where a court order cannot be obtained without endangering the purpose of the measure.
6. FPD, YEDDE and FIU.
7. SAT and PFF can gather and analyse all documents and information related to the commission of criminal tax offences, as well as request, obtain and analyse information from third parties.
8. Outside of tax information, AT relies on the Custom Investigation Service, Police, and the Anti-Corruption Prosecutor to obtain documents from third parties.
9. SECA.
10. Restriction for the cantonal tax administrations: not from Banks directly.
11. ATO.
12. STA-TFIU.

47.   It is noted that this particular investigatory power may have the same purpose as the civil powers of tax examiners and tax auditors when conducting a civil tax examination, which is to obtain information. Since procedural safeguards should apply once a civil examination becomes a criminal investigation, in order to protect a suspect's rights it is important to identify the point at which that line is crossed (see Principle 10). In some jurisdictions civil actions need to cease at this point, while in others civil powers to obtain information for the purposes of the civil examination / audit may still be deployed and may run parallel to a criminal investigation.

48.   However, deploying civil powers for the purposes of the criminal investigation may constitute an abuse of powers and any evidence obtained may be inadmissible in court. Procedural safeguards are of particular importance under the organisational "Model 1" referred to above, where the tax administration conducts civil examinations or audits and also has the authority to conduct criminal investigations. In such a model it is important to take measures or implement an organisational structure or standard operating procedure that prevents interference of civil audits / examinations with criminal investigations to prevent an abuse of powers occurring.

Search powers

49.   This investigative power refers to the search of property and the ability to search and seize physical evidence such as books and records and other materials that may be evidence of a tax crime. This power

generally also allows the investigating authority to use reasonable force to enter the property if needed. This power is available in survey respondents as follows:

Table 3.2. Search powers

Full direct powers Agency responsible for tax crime investigation can be authorised to exercise the power itself			Indirect powers via another agency Agency responsible for tax crime investigation can seek assistance of another agency to exercise the power on its behalf	Not available
Argentina	Georgia	The Netherlands	Australia[7]	Switzerland[9]
Australia[1]	Germany	New Zealand	Honduras	
Austria	Greece[3]	Norway	Italy	
Azerbaijan	Hungary	South Africa	Sweden[8]	
Canada	Iceland	Spain[4]		
Colombia	Ireland	Sweden[5]		
Costa Rica	Israel	Switzerland[6]		
Brazil	Italy	United Kingdom		
Czech Republic[2]	Japan	United States		
Finland	Korea			
France	Mexico			

1. AFP.
2. Police.
3. FPD, YEDDE and FIU.
4. Requests are channeled through the Anti-Corruption Prosecutor and the Customs Investigation Service or the police.
5. SECA.
6. Federal tax administration or a public prosecutor.
7. ATO.
8. STA-TFIU.
9. Cantonal tax administrations.

50.   Search powers should be accompanied by corresponding safeguards that respect a person's right to privacy and to be free from "unreasonable" search. As such, search powers may be limited by a requirement that there are reasonable grounds to believe that a crime has been committed and that procedural authorisations be obtained such as a search warrant.

Power to intercept mail and telecommunications

51.   This refers to the power to review a person's communications, including e-mails, on-line chats, social media, tracking devices and dial number recorders (devices which record incoming and outgoing telephone numbers), keyboard loggers, internet routing addressing, communications using the dark web and many other types of interceptions. This can be an important source of information to establish further inculpatory or exculpatory evidence, to establish a basis to obtain a search warrant, to identify potential search locations, associated persons and co-conspirators to the crime, and to identify criminal assets. Experience from jurisdictions shows that the power to intercept communications varies, as it is a relatively intrusive power and which may be used only in the most serious cases. This power is available in survey respondents as follows:

Table 3.3. Power to Intercept Mail and Telecommunications

Full direct powers Agency responsible for tax crime investigation can be authorised to exercise the power itself		Indirect powers via another agency Agency responsible for tax crime investigation can seek assistance of another agency to exercise the power on its behalf		Not available	
Argentina	Hungary[3]	Australia[4]	Honduras	Chile	Switzerland
Australia[1]	Italy	Brazil	Iceland	Costa Rica[11]	United States
Austria	Mexico	Costa Rica[5]	Israel[9]	Ireland	
Azerbaijan	The Netherlands	Czech Republic[6]	Italy	Japan	
Brazil	United Kingdom	France	Spain	Korea	
Canada		Germany	South Africa	Norway	
Colombia		Georgia[7]	Sweden[10]	New Zealand[12]	
Greece[2]		Greece[8]			

1. AFP in respect of telecommunications.
2. FIU.
3. NTCA.
4. ATO.
5. The Prosecutor's Office can request that the Judicial Investigation Agency (*Organismo de Investigación Judicial; OIJ*) conduct interception of mail and telecommunications but must first receive authorisation from a judge.
6. Police.
7. LEPL Operational-Technical Agency.
8. FPD and YEDDE.
9. ITA has full powers to intercept mail and telecommunications, however a court order is required.
10. Prosecutors on SECA can order police officers to assist in all kind of cases. TFIU cannot act on its own. The unit has to go through the prosecutor.
11. Civil investigators do not have the power to intercept communications.
12. Able to open mail that is found at premises during a search, and obtain existing telecommunications data from third party service providers using powers.

Power to search and seize computer hardware, software, cell phones and digital media

52.   Tax crime investigators may need to search and seize evidence which is in digital form, and be able to do so in a forensically sound manner. While the search powers to obtain evidence referred to above focusses on the search and seizure of physical evidence, this investigative power is focused on the ability to secure digital evidence such as e-mails, text messages, electronic documents and banking records. This type of evidence may be held within computer hardware or software, tablets, cell phones, or any number of electronic storage media including storage in the cloud. For some jurisdictions, this may be an area where the description of investigatory powers in the law has not yet caught up with the rapidly changing digital landscape, and may need to be reformed. This power is available in survey respondents as follows:

Table 3.4. Power to Search and Seize Computer Hardware, Software, Cell Phones and Digital Media

Full direct powers Agency responsible for tax crime investigation can be authorised to exercise the power itself			Indirect powers via another agency Agency responsible for tax crime investigation can seek assistance of another agency to exercise the power on its behalf	Not available
Australia[1]	Georgia	Mexico	Argentina	
Austria	Germany	The Netherlands	Australia[6]	
Azerbaijan	Greece[3]	New Zealand	Czech Republic[7]	
Brazil	Hungary	Norway	Chile	
Canada	Iceland	South Africa	Honduras	

Czech Republic[2]	Ireland	Spain	Israel	
Chile	Israel	Sweden[4]	Sweden[8]	
Colombia	Italy	Switzerland[5]	Switzerland[9]	
Costa Rica	Japan	United Kingdom		
France	Korea	United States		

Note:

1. AFP
2. Police; appeal to delivering of a thing, seizure of a thing.
3. FPD, YEDDE and FIU
4. SECA
5. Federal tax administration or a public prosecutor
6. ATO
7. Police
8. STA-TFIU
9. Cantonal tax administrations

53.   This power has become essential given the increasing use of technology to commit tax crimes and transfer of criminal proceeds.

Box 3.1. Example of successful implementation of tax crime strategy in the Netherlands: Crypto mixers

In 2020, the FIOD and the Public Prosecution Service took one of the largest online mixers for cryptocurrencies offline, named *Bestmixer.io*. This operation deals a severe blow to the concealment of criminal flows of money by mixing cryptocurrencies such as bitcoins. Six operational servers have been dismantled and seized in the Netherlands and Luxembourg. The investigation was conducted in close co-operation with the Dutch Digital Intrusion Team (DIGIT), Europol and the authorities in Luxembourg, France and Latvia. In June 2018 the Financial Advanced Cyber Team (FACT) of the FIOD started the investigation under the supervision of the National Public Prosecutor's Office for Serious Fraud and Environmental Crime and Asset Confiscation. The reason for the investigation was a report from cyber security company McAfee.

The investigation gathered information regarding transactions between customers and *Bestmixer.io*. The customers are located all over the world, especially in the US, Germany and the Netherlands. The FIOD analyzed the information together with Europol. After that the data was shared with other countries. On the anonymous part of the Internet, the darknet, cryptocurrencies are a regular means of payment and are often used as means of payment in the criminal world. A crypto mixing service is an online service that makes it possible to conceal the origin or destination of cryptocurrencies. This service is used to split up cryptocurrencies against payment of a commission, after which they are mixed together in a different combination.

People who use a mixing service probably do so to increase their anonymity. The investigation so far shows that many of the mixed cryptocurrencies have a criminal origin or destination. In these cases, the mixer was probably used to conceal and launder criminal flows of money. The total turnover of darknet markets amounts to approx. USD 800 million per year. It is believed that a large part of the payments via the darknet take place via mixers in order to launder the criminal (crypto) money.

Bestmixer.io is one of the three largest mixing services for cryptocurrencies and offered services for mixing the cryptocurrencies bitcoins, bitcoin cash and litecoins. The service started in May 2018 and achieved a turnover of at least USD 200 million (approx. 25 000 bitcoins) in a year's time and guaranteed that the customers would remain anonymous. The operation against *Bestmixer.io* is a significant and important step in the fight against criminal flows of money in general and virtual criminal flows of money in particular.

54.	During a physical search of a home or office, documents can be reviewed in a manner that quickly indicates whether or not they are covered by the search warrant and relevant to the investigation. However, digital media may contain hundreds of thousands of e-mails, documents and text messages, created over many years, and not necessarily related to the tax crime. It is therefore challenging, if not impossible, to determine during the onsite search whether or not a particular piece of electronic information is covered by the search warrant and its relevance. Therefore, the search may include digitally copying or imaging the data that is held, and examining the contents in a forensic lab in order to determine which pieces of the information are within the scope of the search warrant and relevant to the case under investigation.

55.	For example, in Australia, police have the power to operate electronic equipment found at a search warrant premises to access data (including data not held on the premises). If the data accessed is evidential material, it can be copied and removed by operating the equipment or, if it is not practicable to do so, seizing the equipment. An item found at the warrant premises may be removed for up to 14 days for examination or processing in order to determine if it may be seized under the warrant, if it is significantly more practicable to do so having regard to timeliness and the cost of examining or processing the item and the availability of expert assistance. This has proven particularly useful in large complex tax and fraud investigations, in which large amounts of data must be searched on the digital media in order to identify the relevant evidence.

56.	There may also be legal challenges connected with the search and seizure of digital data in computers and other electronic devices. Personal data in an electronic device may not be relevant to the suspected tax crime, or may contain data protected by a legal professional privilege. This may require that the search is carefully governed to ensure it is limited to the terms of the authorisation. There may also be legal challenges connected with the search and seizure of computers and other electronic devices. This may be particularly pertinent in cases where the search powers contained in the law refer explicitly to searches or seizure of physical documents, or where a person challenges a search of digital media on the basis that it is overly broad and goes beyond the terms of the search authority or could include privileged documents.

57.	Based on survey data, the most commonly reported challenge agencies face in the search and seizure of digital media involves data stored outside the jurisdiction or in the cloud, as their legislation only allows for the search of data which is locally stored. Jurisdictions also noted the challenges of searching large amounts of data, data protected by encrypted passwords, and data that is unable to be accessed because of secrecy laws. Possible solutions mentioned by jurisdictions included the development of an IT system able to sort the main relevant data and a special IT training for professionals in tax crime investigation.

Power to interview

58.	This investigative power refers to the ability to interview suspects, accused persons and witnesses to obtain information.

59.	The power to interview is generally a power to initiate an interview, rather than a power to compel a person to speak or to provide information during that interview. A distinction should be made between suspects, accused persons and witnesses. Whether or not a suspect provides information during the interview relies on the voluntary co-operation of that suspect. This reflects a suspects' right to remain silent and right to protection from self-incrimination. For this purpose, suspects should be cautioned at the start of the interview. With respect to witnesses, although they do not have the same right to remain silent, legal privileges and professional secrecy provisions may be applicable, e.g., for family members or certain professions. This power is available in survey respondents as follows:

Table 3.5. Power to Interview

Full direct powers Agency responsible for tax crime investigation can be authorised to exercise the power itself			Indirect powers via another agency Agency responsible for tax crime investigation can seek assistance of another agency to exercise the power on its behalf	Not available
Argentina	Germany	New Zealand	Australia[4]	Ireland
Australia[1]	Greece[3]	Norway	Greece[5]	
Austria	Honduras	South Africa		
Azerbaijan	Hungary	Spain		
Brazil	Iceland	Sweden		
Canada	Israel	Switzerland		
Chile	Italy	United Kingdom		
Colombia	Japan	United States		
Costa Rica	Korea			
Czech Republic[2]	Mexico			
Georgia	The Netherlands			

1. AFP and ACIC.
2. Police.
3. FPD and YEDDE.
4. ATO.
5. FIU.

60.   Jurisdictions may also have powers to compel the giving of information, such as inquiry powers which can subpoena potential witnesses before a tribunal or court to answer questions under oath. This can be a particularly powerful tool where a person is unwilling to provide information, such as where contractual duties of confidentiality exist. However, legal privileges and the right of a suspect to remain silent continue to apply. This power is available in survey respondents as follows:

Table 3.6. Powers to Compel the Giving of Information

Full direct powers Agency responsible for tax crime investigation can be authorised to exercise the power itself			Indirect powers via another agency Agency responsible for tax crime investigation can seek assistance of another agency to exercise the power on its behalf	Not Available
Australia[1]	Georgia	Norway	Argentina	Chile
Austria	Germany	South Africa	Australia[3]	Greece
Azerbaijan	Hungary	Spain		Ireland
Brazil	Honduras	Sweden		Japan
Canada	Iceland	Switzerland[2]		Korea
Colombia	Italy	United Kingdom		
Costa Rica	The Netherlands	United States		
Czech Republic	Mexico			
France	New Zealand			

1. ACIC.
2. With restrictions.
3. ATO.

Power to conduct covert surveillance

61.   This power refers to the covert monitoring of the movements, conversations and other activities of a suspect to identify co-conspirators or witnesses, locate evidence in order to obtain search warrants, identify assets being used in perpetrating the tax crime or assets that are the proceeds of crime. Covert

surveillance can include observation of a person in private places such as within a person's home or vehicle as well as observation of a person in public. Covert surveillance can be particularly relevant for investigating any tax crimes involving organised crime. This power is available in survey respondents as follows:

Table 3.7. Power to Conduct Covert Surveillance

Full direct powers Agency responsible for tax crime investigation can be authorised to exercise the power itself		Indirect powers via another agency Agency responsible for tax crime investigation can seek assistance of another agency to exercise the power on its behalf	Not available
Australia[1]	Ireland	Argentina	Chile
Austria	Italy	Australia[7]	Costa Rica
Azerbaijan	Japan	Canada[8]	Germany
Brazil	Mexico	Costa Rica[9]	Israel
Canada[2]	The Netherlands	Czech Republic[10]	Korea
Colombia	New Zealand	Iceland[11]	South Africa
Czech Republic[3]	Sweden[5]	Honduras	Switzerland
France	Switzerland[6]	Norway	
Georgia	United Kingdom	Spain	
Greece[4]	United States		
Hungary			

1. AFP.
2. Static surveillance is the primary surveillance tactic employed by CRA investigators. CRA investigators are not trained in mobile surveillance and are prohibited from undertaking any form of surveillance involving a motor vehicle. Mobile surveillance may be contracted out to the Canada Border Services Agency, Royal Canadian Mounted Police (RCMP) or other trained law enforcement agencies.
3. Police; full direct powers for surveillance of persons and things without recording.
4. FPD, YEDDE and FIU.
5. SECA has full direct powers to conduct covert surveillance.
6. FCA.
7. ATO.
8. Static surveillance is the primary surveillance tactic employed by CRA investigators. While mobile surveillance by CRA is prohibited; it may ask federal law enforcement agencies to operate on its behalf.
9. OIJ.
10. Police.
11. If necessary for an investigation, this would be conducted by the Police.

Power to conduct undercover operations

62.   This power refers to the ability to conduct an undercover operation, where an enforcement officer takes on a different identity in order to obtain information and evidence. This investigative tool may be particularly important in the investigation of ongoing serious crimes such as identifying enablers of tax crimes and other financial crimes where organised crime is involved. The type of information that can be obtained using this investigative power is similar to that sought through covert surveillance, including establishing the identity of co-conspirators and location of assets.

63.   The distinction between conducting covert surveillance to obtain this information and conducting an undercover operation is the embedding of the undercover officer, or at least direct contact of the undercover officer, with the criminal organisation for the purposes of gaining their trust to obtain information. The contact of the officer may be physical interactions or digital interactions such as on online platforms. This power is available in survey respondents as follows:

Table 3.8. Power to Conduct Undercover Operations

Full direct powers		Indirect powers via another agency	Not available
Agency responsible for tax crime investigation can be authorised to exercise the power itself		Agency responsible for tax crime investigation can seek assistance of another agency to exercise the power on its behalf	
Australia[1]	Mexico	Argentina	Argentina[8]
Austria	The Netherlands	Australia[3]	Azerbaijan
Colombia	New Zealand	Brazil	Chile
Costa Rica	Sweden	Canada[4]	Ireland
France	United Kingdom	Czech Republic[5]	Italy
Germany	United States	Georgia[6]	Japan
Greece[2]		Honduras	Korea
Hungary		Iceland[7]	South Africa
		Norway	Switzerland
		Spain	

1. AFP.
2. FPD and FIU.
3. ATO.
4. Criminal Investigations may approach the local RCMP detachment to undertake an undercover operation on behalf of CRA. CRA investigators may themselves undertake only the least sophisticated and non-obtrusive types of undercover operations such as visiting a restaurant, bar or office; to obtain information or documents that are readily available to all clients such as bills, invoices or pamphlets.
5. Police.
6. LEPL Operational-Technical Agency.
7. This would be conducted by the Police.
8. Undercover operations are not usually conducted in cases of tax crimes. The law allows for special investigative techniques (such as undercover operations) to be used in cases of customs offences and money laundering offences, which may be connected to the laundering of proceeds of tax crimes.

64.   Undercover operations are costly and can be dangerous, and require expert skills and training of the officers involved. As such, undercover operations are likely to be used less frequently. As with the other investigative powers noted within Principle 3, issues of suspect's rights and protections such as privacy and issues related to entrapment must be safeguarded by following the correct legal procedures governing the use of these powers.

Power to arrest a person

65.   The power to arrest a person refers to the power to stop, restrain and take a person into custody, often for the purpose of formally charging them with an offence. The power to arrest a person and to take them into custody (with or without restrictions) can be critical during a tax crime investigation, so as to prevent them from influencing other suspects or witnesses as well as when there is a risk of flight by the accused or suspect, or to restrain this person in order to prevent them from committing additional crimes. This power is available in survey respondents as follows:

Table 3.9. Power to Arrest a Person

Full direct powers		Indirect powers via another agency	Not available
Agency responsible for tax crime investigation can be authorised to exercise the power itself		Agency responsible for tax crime investigation can seek assistance of another agency to exercise the power on its behalf	
Australia[1]	Sweden[4]	Argentina	Australia[7]
Austria	Mexico	Canada	Azerbaijan
Colombia	The Netherlands	Czech Republic[5]	Germany
Costa Rica[2]	Norway	Iceland	Chile

France	United Kingdom	Japan	Costa Rica
Georgia	United States	Spain	Greece[8]
Greece[3]		Switzerland[6]	New Zealand
Honduras			Korea
Ireland			South Africa
Italy			Sweden[9]
			Switzerland[10]

1. AFP.
2. Prosecutor's Office.
3. FPD.
4. SECA.
5. Police.
6. Federal tax administration or a public prosecutor.
7. ATO.
8. FIU.
9. STA-TFIU.
10. Cantonal tax authorities.

66. In some jurisdictions, the arrest and custody of an accused person or suspect also provides continuous availability for interviewing the suspect or accused person for a certain period of time, subject to protections under the law.

67. As is the case with the use of investigative powers by any law enforcement agency, these must be accompanied by safeguards, oversight, and authorisations to ensure that the suspects and accused persons are adequately protected from any potential abuse of these investigative powers (see Principle 10 for more details).

References

OECD (2017), *Effective Inter-Agency Co-Operation in Fighting Tax Crimes and Other Financial Crimes - Third Edition*, OECD Publishing, Paris, https://www.oecd.org/tax/crime/effective-inter-agency-co-operation-in-fighting-tax-crimes-and-other-financial-crimes.htm.   [1]

Principle 4 Have effective powers to freeze, seize and confiscate assets

---

Jurisdictions should have the ability to freeze / seize assets in the course of a tax crime investigation, and the ability to confiscate assets.

Introduction

68.   Freezing or seizing of assets involves "temporarily prohibiting the transfer, conversion, disposition or movement of assets or temporarily assuming custody or control of assets on the basis of an order issued by a court or other competent authority" (UNODC, 2004[1]). Freezing is an action that temporarily suspends rights over the asset and for example, may apply to bank accounts which are fungible. Seizure is an action to temporarily restrain an asset or put it into the custody of the governmentand may apply to physical assets such as a vehicle. Generally, these measures are used to temporarily prevent the movement of assets pending the outcome of a case.

69.   Confiscation of assets, on the other hand, can be defined as "the permanent deprivation of assets by order of a court or other competent authority" (UNODC, 2004[1]). Confiscation (which may be referred to as asset forfeiture) is generally used after the final outcome of a case, as it is a final measure that stops criminals from accessing assets obtained from a crime. Freezing, seizing and confiscation powers must be exercised in accordance with national law, including requirements as to proportionality.

70.   In order to be able to successfully conduct criminal investigations and to ensure that the assets that gave rise to, or are the product of tax crime are adequately secured throughout the investigations, it is important that the investigation agencies can freeze or seize such assets for the duration of the investigation and the criminal procedure. As noted above, in the investigation of tax offences, being able to interrupt the movement of financial assets can be essential in identifying or preventing an offence. In addition, agencies should have the authority to confiscate assets that gave rise to, or are the product of

tax crimes. This is particularly relevant in fighting tax crimes, as financial assets are easily removed from one jurisdiction to another and can lead to financial losses for governments.

71.   The freezing, seizing and confiscation of assets are necessary in order to prevent the proceeds of a crime from being disposed of or being enjoyed by a suspect, or to preserve physical evidence of a crime. In some jurisdictions, the confiscation or forfeiture of an asset may be a sanction on its own, or a means to ensure pecuniary fines are paid. Freezing, seizing and confiscation disrupts criminal activity by inhibiting access to assets that would have been beneficial to the individual or organisation committing the crime or can prevent the criminal assets from being employed to commit further crimes. The freezing, seizing and confiscating of criminal assets is also a deterrent measure as it can reduce the profitability of committing tax crimes.

72.   The availability of relevant freezing, seizing and confiscation powers amongst survey respondents is set out in the country chapters and below. Throughout this section of the guide, it is noted that the precise circumstances and legal procedures that need to be followed in order to use freezing, seizing or confiscations measures vary. The representation of jurisdictions as having a particular mechanism "available" is not intended to reflect that the mechanism can be used in all investigations of a tax offence, but that the mechanism is available at least in some cases for tax offences and provided that the necessary legal and procedural authorisations have been obtained.

73.   Jurisdictions should ensure that the freezing, seizing and confiscating of assets is possible for both domestic and foreign tax investigations and judgments. The legal power to do so should be in domestic law, or for international cases may be undertaken in response to a request for mutual legal assistance in accordance with international agreements such as a mutual legal assisstance treaty(MLAT). (See Principle 9 for more details). Survey respondents have the legal ability to apply seizing and confiscation powers in respect of foreign tax investigations and foreign court judgments (e.g., following an MLAT request) as follows:

Table 4.1. Survey responses: Availability of seizing and confiscation powers in respect of foreign tax matters

Available			Not available
Argentina	France	The Netherlands[1]	Honduras
Australia	Georgia	New Zealand	
Austria	Germany	Norway	
Azerbaijan	Greece	South Africa	
Brazil	Hungary	Spain	
Canada	Israel	Sweden	
Colombia	Italy	Switzerland	
Chile	Japan	United Kingdom	
Costa Rica	Korea	United States	
Czech Republic	Mexico		

1. In the Netherlands, courts are able to execute foreign states' confiscation orders that forfeit the property to the relevant foreign state, based on reciprocity, and have done so in practice. However, courts cannot enforce a foreign state freezing or seizure order in criminal tax matters.

74.   The available mechanisms for the freezing, seizing and confiscating of assets will vary between jurisdictions, but the mechanisms described below may be relevant to consider. Whether all of these mechanisms are available in a particular jurisdiction or in a particular agency will depend on the organisational structure for investigating tax offences and taking enforcement actions, as well as the particular legal system which may not permit certain measures which involve the deprivation of assets.

Rapid freezing of assets

75.   Speed can be essential when it comes to freezing and seizing assets, as criminals can quickly transfer funds out of the agencies' reach or dispose of property if they become aware that the criminal investigation agencies are investigating them. The legal authority and operational capacity to freeze assets rapidly in urgent cases is relevant, for example, where the loss of property is imminent. Agencies should generally be able to execute rapid freezing orders within 24 and 48 hours. This power is available in respect of tax crimes in survey respondents as follows:

Table 4.2. Survey responses: Availability of powers for rapid freezing orders

Available		Not available	Indirect powers via another agency
Argentina	Japan	Azerbaijan	Brazil
Australia	Hungary	Canada	Italy
Austria	Mexico	Chile	Korea
Colombia[1]	The Netherlands	Greece	Chile
Costa Rica	South Africa	Honduras	
Czech Republic	Spain	Israel	
Finland	Sweden	New Zealand	
France	Switzerland	Norway	
Georgia	United Kingdom		
Germany	United States		
Greece[2]			

1. Limited to protecting potential compensation damages (art. 92 of the Criminal Procedure Code).
2. FIU.

Extended confiscation

76.   This is an action that involves not only confiscating property associated with a specific crime, but also additional property which the court determines constitutes the proceeds of other crimes. This might be useful to effectively tackle organised criminal activities to not only confiscate property associated with a specific crime, but also additional property which the court determines to be the proceeds of other crimes. This power is available in respect of tax crimes in survey respondents as follows:

Table 4.3. Survey responses: Availability of powers for extended confiscation

Available		Not available	Indirect powers via another agency
Argentina	Italy	Azerbaijan	Colombia
Australia	Mexico	Chile	New Zealand
Austria	South Africa	Costa Rica	Japan[2]
Brazil[1]	Spain	Ireland	Korea
Canada	Sweden	Georgia	
Czech Republic	Switzerland	Greece	
France	The Netherlands		
Germany	Norway		
Honduras	United Kingdom		
Hungary	United States		
Israel			

1. Only to crimes with maximum sanction over six years of imprisonment. Thereby, it is not applied to tax crimes.
2. While Japan notes that it does not have powers to confiscate assets based on convictions for tax crimes, it may do so on money laundering convictions where tax crime was a predicate offence.

Value-based confiscations

77.   This is a method of confiscation that enables a court to impose a pecuniary liability equivalent to the amount of the criminal proceeds. This applies once the court determines the amount of the benefit accruing directly or indirectly to an individual from criminal conduct, and the order is realisable against any asset of the individual. This power is available in respect of tax crimes in survey respondents as follows:

Table 4.4. Survey responses: Availability of powers for value-based confiscations

Available			Not available	Indirect powers via another agency
Australia	Hungary	Sweden	Argentina	Italy
Austria	Israel	Switzerland	Chile	Korea
Azerbaijan	Japan	The Netherlands	Colombia	
Brazil	Mexico	United Kingdom	Greece	
Canada	Norway	United States	Honduras	
Czech Republic	Germany		New Zealand	
France	South Africa		Switzerland	
Georgia	Spain			

Third party confiscations

78.   This is a measure made to deprive someone other than the offender – the third party – of criminal property. This applies where that third party is in possession of assets which are knowingly transferred to him/her by the offender to frustrate confiscation. Third party confiscation can alleviate the risk that an agency could be frustrated by the suspect transferring criminal property to a third party to avoid confiscation. This power is available in respect of tax crimes in survey respondents as follows:

Table 4.5. Survey responses: Availability of powers for third party confiscations

Available		Not available		Indirect powers via another agency
Argentina	Hungary	Azerbaijan	Sweden	Brazil
Australia	Israel	Canada	United Kingdom	Italy
Austria	Japan	Chile		New Zealand
Costa Rica	Mexico	Colombia		Korea
Czech Republic	The Netherlands	Greece		
France	Spain	Norway		
Germany	Switzerland			
Georgia	United States			

Non-conviction based confiscation

79.   Non-conviction based confiscation is the power to seize assets without a criminal trial and conviction and is an enforcement action taken against the asset itself and not the individual. It is a separate action from any criminal proceeding and requires proof that the property is the proceeds or an instrumentality of crime. In some jurisdictions, the criminal conduct must be established using a standard of proof of the balance of probabilities, which reduces the burden for the agency and means that it may be possible to obtain the assets even where there is insufficient evidence to support a criminal conviction. This power is available in respect of tax crimes in survey respondents as follows:

Table 4.6. Survey responses: Availability of powers for non-conviction based confiscation

Available		Not available		Indirect powers via another agency
Australia	Mexico	Argentina	South Africa	Italy
Austria	Norway	Azerbaijan	Spain	New Zealand
Czech Republic	Spain[2]	Brazil	Sweden	Korea
Costa Rica[1]	United Kingdom	Canada	The Netherlands	
Germany	United States	Chile	Switzerland	
Israel		Colombia		
		France[3]		
		Georgia		
		Greece		
		Honduras		
		Hungary		

1. Costa Rica only allows non-conviction based confiscations if the case is being treated as one of organised crime.
2. Non-conviction based confiscation can be applied as an exception, under the authorisation of the courts, only where the confiscated asset is perishable, was abandoned by the owner, its conservation costs are greater than the asset itself, its conservation is dangerous for public health or safety, and if it depreciates over time.
3. There is no confiscation procedure in the absence of a criminal conviction (so-called civil confiscation) in French law. However, the non-return of seized property resulting directly or indirectly from the offense can be permitted in certain circumstances.

80.   In order to effectively recover criminal assets, jurisdictions should consider the following:

- Having the necessary governance framework to ensure criminal law enforcement agencies operate transparently and are adequately supervised in connection with the handling of assets to ensure integrity;

- Having the necessary investigative, legal and operational expertise;

- Putting in place a clear organisational structure to manage asset cases. Given that these cases can require specialised investigative and legal expertise which may be located across different agencies, it can be efficient to put in place a specialised multi-agency unit with trained practitioners and adequate resources focussing on asset recovery;

- Ensuring that the rights of suspects are protected during an asset recovery process;

- Having a process to safely manage the assets; and

- Efficiently using international co-operation, given that asset recovery cases can be complex and involve criminal assets located in foreign jurisdictions.

References

UNODC (2004), *United Nations Convention Against Transnational Organized Crime and The Protocols Thereto*, United Nations, New York, http://www.unodc.org/documents/treaties/UNTOC/Publications/TOC%20Convention/TOCebook-e.pdf.   [1]

Principle 5 Put in place an organisational structure with defined responsibilities

A Jurisdiction should have an organisational model with defined responsibilities for fighting tax crime and other financial crime.

Introduction

81.   A range of organisational models exist for allocating the responsibilities for investigating and prosecuting tax crimes. The model adopted in a particular jurisdiction is likely to take into account the jurisdiction's history, its general structure of law enforcement and its legal system.

82.   Having a clear organisational model is important because it will allow for efficient allocation of responsibilities, which can reduce the risk of duplication of efforts and gaps in law enforcement. A clear organisational structure is also important as it allows for greater transparency and accountability for the use of resources and deployment of strategies. The organisational structure should ensure that the agency responsible for the investigation and prosecution of tax crimes is independent of personal or political interests, and is also held accountable for exercising its functions with fairness and integrity.

83.   Understanding the particular organisational structure that is in place in the jurisdiction is important because it will inform how a jurisdiction can best implement a number of the other Global Principles. For example, the organisational structure will affect the design of the overall compliance strategy, the range of investigatory powers that should be granted, allocating the appropriate amount of resources, and devising strategies for inter-agency co-operation and international co-operation.

Table 5.1. Four general organisational models

General Organisational Models for Investigating Tax Crimes			
Model 1	**Model 2**	**Model 3**	**Model 4**
The tax administration has responsibility for directing and conducting investigations, often through a specialist criminal investigations division. The public prosecutor's office does not have a direct role in investigations, though a prosecutor may provide advice to investigators with respect to matters such as legal process and the laws of evidence.	The tax administration has responsibility for conducting investigations, under the direction of the public prosecutor or, exceptionally, examining judges.	A specialist tax agency, under the supervision of the Ministry of Finance but outside the tax administration, has responsibility for conducting investigations, which may involve public prosecutors.	The police or public prosecutor has responsibility for conducting investigations.

84.   However, in some jurisdictions a combination of models may be used depending on the circumstances of the case, or another model altogether may be in place.

Box 5.1. A new Tax Crime Unit in Colombia

Colombia's National Directorate of Taxes and Customs (DIAN) is a participant in the OECD-UNDP pilot project "Tax Inspectors Without Borders for Criminal Investigation" (TIWB-CI). TIWB-CI aims to build capacity in participating jurisdictions to help fight tax crimes more effectively. As part of this programme, a self-assessment exercise was conducted through the OECD's "Tax Crime Investigation Maturity Model", to ascertain the gaps in current capacity. The Action Plan prepared by the OECD, following the self-assessment process, recommended the creation of a new tax crime investigation unit within DIAN to address governance gaps and institutional shortcomings.

Following this, Colombia issued Decree 1742 of 22 December 2020, creating a new tax crime unit within DIAN. This new unit will be in charge of reporting suspicions of crimes, including tax evasion, fraud and smuggling, to the law enforcement agency, participate in joint investigative teams, and engage in domestic and cross-border exchanges of information for criminal investigation purposes.

---

85.   Whichever organisational model is used, it is important that the agency or agencies responsible for investigating and prosecuting tax crimes have clearly defined responsibilities. This will help to ensure that responsibility for all aspects of fighting tax crimes are clearly designated, as well as to reduce the possibility of inefficient duplication of responsibilities. This should be accompanied by clear governance arrangements (such as clear decision-making responsibility, accountability and supervision), and the appropriate investigative powers (see Principle 3) and adequate resources (see Principle 6). The organisational structure should also be clearly aligned with the models for inter-agency co-operation (see Principle 8).

86.   For more information, including on the organisational models used by customs, AML, anti-corruption and other law enforcement authorities, see the OECD (2017), Effective Inter-agency Co-operation in Fighting Tax Crimes and Other Financial Crimes, Third Edition (OECD, 2017[1]).

References

OECD (2017), *Effective Inter-Agency Co-Operation in Fighting Tax Crimes and Other Financial Crimes - Third Edition*, OECD Publishing, Paris, http://www.oecd.org/tax/crime/effective-inter-agency-co-operation-in-fighting-tax-crimes-and-other-financial-crimes.htm. [1]

Principle 6 Provide adequate resources for tax crime investigation

---

Tax crime investigation agencies should have adequate resources.

Introduction

87.   Whatever the organisational model, sufficient resources should be allocated to investigate and take enforcement action in respect of tax crimes. The level and type of resources will vary in accordance with the overall budgetary constraints and other budgetary priorities for the jurisdiction. In particular the type of resources needed may vary depending on the nature, scale and developmental stage of the economy. For example, it may be more urgent to build the legal and physical infrastructure before acquiring advanced analytical and technology tools.

88.   Moreover, the allocation of resources to different functions within the agency responsible for conducting tax crime investigations will vary depending on other factors, such as the strategic priorities and the organisational structure.

89.   Recognising these circumstances, the important resources for agencies fighting tax crimes are set out below.

Financial resources

90.   This means having the budget and funding to pay for the needs of the agency. The average budget for surveyed jurisdictions for which data was available was as follows:

Table 6.1. Survey responses: Average annual budget over 2015 and 2018 allocated for the investigation of tax crimes in Euro equivalent (does not include budget for prosecution)

Austria	11 400 000	Japan	7 035 435
Canada	47 100 000	Netherlands[1]	128 000 000
Estonia	3 000 000	South Africa	10 000 000
Georgia	4 472 517	United States[2]	493 557 000

1. Figure includes the whole Fiscal Information and Investigation Service (FIOD).
2. Majority of this budget is used for tax crime investigations.

91.   Most surveyed jurisdictions indicated that the allocation of their budget was not dependent on meeting defined performance measures, even where performance targets had been agreed. From the survey, having pre-defined performance targets was uncommon. A minority of responding jurisdictions noted that performance targets had been identified, which included a minimum number of concluded investigations, number or percentage of investigations leading to prosecution, surplus earning, target time to complete an investigation, and revenue collection target.

92.   Some surveyed jurisdictions were able to estimate the return on investment from the tax crime investigation function, as follows.

Box 6.1. Estimated return on investment from tax criminal investigation budget

- In Georgia, for every Georgian lari invested on tax crime investigation, the investigation service collected GEL 1.88 in 2018 (**88% return**).

- In Mexico, for every dollar spent in tax crime prosecutions in 2019, there was a return of USD 16 (**1 600% return**).

- In Spain, in the years 2015 to 2019, for every euro spent in tax investigations, the tax agency collected EUR 11.51 (**return of 1 151%**).

- Switzerland, at the federal level, estimates a return of investment in tax crime investigations of 20 times the total costs of its staff (**2 000% return** on staff costs).

Human resources

93.   This means having staff with the appropriate knowledge, expertise, training and skills. Human resources are likely to have a significant impact on the efficient use of financial resources. This includes having a sufficient number of staff working on tax crime investigations. Staff numbers in the area responsible for tax crime investigations in surveyed jurisdictions, where data was available, was as follows:

Table 6.2. Average number of full time equivalent staff responsible for tax crime investigations in 2018

Country	No. of full-time staff	Country	No. of full-time staff
Argentina	83	Greece	1 782
Austria	145	Honduras	45
Azerbaijan	40	Hungary	1 179
Canada	564	Ireland	2 000
Chile	56	Israel	500
Colombia	132	Japan	1 494

Country	No. of full-time staff	Country	No. of full-time staff
Costa Rica	246	Mexico	60
Czech Republic	300	Spain	4 800
France	105	Sweden	200
Georgia	394	Switzerland	22
Germany	2 454	United States	2 200

Note: Figures for Argentina represent the number of prosecutors in charge of tax crimes. Figures for Austria represent the Tax Crime Investigation Unit. Figures for Azerbaijan represent DPTIC. Figures for Canada represent the CID-CRA. Figures for Chile represent the Departments of Tax Crimes and of Criminal Judicial Defense of SII in 2020. Figures for Costa Rica represent the number of officials in charge of tax audits. Figures for the Czech Republic include averages for the Serious Economic Crime and Corruption Command of NOCA, the Risk Management Division and the FCD in 2015. Figures for France represent the Office of the Prosecutor for Financial Crimes, BNRDF and SEJF. Figures for Germany represent the number of tax inspectors. Figures for Hungary represent the Criminal Investigation Service of NTCA in 2020. Figures for Honduras represent the criminal investigations division of SAR. Figures for Hungary represent the Criminal Investigation Service of NTCA in 2020. Figures for Israel represent an average of the number of staff in charge of criminal investigations at ITA. Figures for Japan repesent the number of staff dedicated to tax crime investigations at NTA. Figures for Mexico represent lawyers at PFF. Figures for Spain represent AEAT. Figures for Sweden represent the average for 2015-19 for STA/TFIU. Figures for Switzerland represent an average for DPAI/FTA. Figures for the United States represent investigators and supervisory positions at IRS-CI.

94.   Having the necessary human resources also includes ensuring that staff have the appropriate skills and knowledge to conduct complex financial investigations. This includes two aspects: having staff with expertise in all relevant fields; and providing ongoing training on emerging risks, investigative tools and skills.

95.   The need to ensure that the agency has the necessary expertise in all relevant fields reflects the fact that financial crime investigations demand specialist knowledge and know-how and that a range of specialist skills may be needed within an investigation. All financial investigators should have a certain basic level of financial knowledge and skills such as practical investigation techniques, case management and intelligence collection. In addition, more specialised financial investigators will be needed, such as accountants, asset recovery specialists, cyber experts and forensic experts.

Training

96.   Training should be continuous and available for all staff at every level of experience and should include areas such as legal knowledge, emerging risks, investigative techniques, interview techniques, using and leveraging technology solutions, management skills, and working in cross-agency and international investigations. Where possible, training should include practical training drawn from real-life cases, as well as incorporating joint training sessions with investigators, prosecutors, tax authorities and other relevant stakeholders to create greater awareness of the possibilities for inter-agency co-operation. Undertaking international training can also be beneficial in sharing different approaches and creating a network of professionals that can enhance international co-operation.

Infrastructure resources

97.   A range of physical tools are required to conduct tax crime investigations effectively, such as forensic tools, administrative equipment (including for enforcement actions), the ability to securely handle evidence, and effective communication platforms among other things.

Organisational resources

98.   Robust organisational and strategic resources are needed to conduct the work and use the resources efficiently, as well as a network of inter-agency relationships.

Data and technology resources

99.   It is important that investigators have access to relevant data and intelligence, as well as the hardware and software to analyse it. In terms of the data and intelligence required, this should include access to tax and other revenue information, bank account information, real estate information and commercial and company information. In terms of the technology resources, this includes computers, IT systems, smartphones, and data storage systems as well as the analytical tools to establish links, patterns and risks amongst different sources of data (both structured and unstructured data). Increasingly, law enforcement agencies need to have the skills and tools to conduct investigations in response to the increasing digitalisation and globalisation of criminal activity. It is likely that information and data analytics will become even more important over time, and access to a wider range of digital information and analytical tools will be needed. The survey shows that responding jurisdictions have access to a number of databases. Note that not all such databases exist in each jurisdiction. The table below is intended to describe the current approaches taken by different jurisdictions, which depend on the organisational structure, availability and sensitivity of certain data, and without reaching a conclusion as to the effectiveness of such forms of access.

Table 6.3. Survey responses: Access to Government Databases and Registers

	Access on request		Direct access		No access
Company Formation / Ownership Registry	Argentina Australia Canada Colombia Costa Rica Czech Republic[1] Germany	Honduras Japan Mexico New Zealand South Africa United Kingdom United States	Austria Brazil Czech Republic[2] Denmark France Georgia Greece Hungary Iceland Ireland	Israel Italy Korea The Netherlands New Zealand Norway Spain Sweden Switzerland United States	Chile
Land Registry	Australia Canada Costa Rica Denmark France Germany Greece Japan	Korea Mexico New Zealand South Africa Switzerland United Kingdom United States	Austria Brazil Colombia Czech Republic Georgia Honduras Hungary Iceland Ireland	Italy Israel The Netherlands New Zealand Norway Spain Sweden United States	Chile
Registry Of Citizens[3]	Australia Costa Rica Germany Greece Ireland Japan Korea	Mexico New Zealand South Africa Spain Switzerland United Kingdom United States	Argentina Austria Brazil Chile Colombia Czech Republic Denmark France Georgia	Honduras Hungary Iceland Israel Italy The Netherlands Norway Sweden United States	Canada

	Access on request		Direct access		No access
Tax Databases	Brazil Colombia Costa Rica Denmark France	Hungary Mexico Norway Sweden	Argentina Australia Austria Canada Chile Czech Republic[4] France[5] Georgia Germany Greece Honduras Iceland Ireland	Israel Italy Japan Korea The Netherlands New Zealand Norway South Africa Spain Sweden Switzerland United Kingdom United States	
Customs Databases	Australia Brazil Canada Colombia Denmark France Germany Greece[6] Hungary	Japan Korea Mexico New Zealand Norway Sweden Switzerland[7] United States	Argentina Austria Czech Republic[8] Georgia Greece[9] Honduras Iceland Ireland Israel	Italy The Netherlands South Africa Spain Switzerland[10] United Kingdom	Chile Costa Rica
Police Databases	Argentina Australia France Germany Greece[11] Honduras Ireland Israel Japan	Korea Mexico New Zealand South Africa Switzerland[12] United Kingdom United States	Argentina Austria Azerbaijan Brazil Canada Colombia Costa Rica Czech Republic Denmark	France[13] Georgia Greece[14] Hungary Italy The Netherlands Norway Sweden[15]	Chile Iceland Norway Spain Switzerland
Judicial Databases	Australia Austria Canada Czech Republic Georgia Germany Greece Honduras Hungary	Ireland Korea Mexico The Netherlands New Zealand South Africa United Kingdom United States	Argentina Brazil Colombia Costa Rica France Iceland Italy Japan New Zealand	Norway Switzerland United States Israel	Chile Norway Spain Sweden Switzerland
STR Databases	Austria Brazil[16] Czech Republic Germany Greece[17] Georgia Honduras Hungary Israel	Italy Japan Korea Mexico The Netherlands New Zealand Spain Sweden	Australia Denmark Greece[18] Ireland Japan South Africa	United Kingdom United States	Argentina Canada Chile Colombia Costa Rica France Iceland Norway Switzerland

	Access on request		Direct access		No access
Domestic Bank Account Databases	Argentina Australia Brazil Colombia Czech Republic France Georgia Germany Greece Honduras Hungary Iceland	Ireland Israel Japan Korea Mexico Norway South Africa Spain Switzerland United Kingdom United States	Austria Azerbaijan Costa Rica France[19] Italy The Netherlands		Argentina Canada Chile Sweden
Car Registry	Australia Canada Germany Honduras Japan Korea	Mexico New Zealand South Africa Switzerland[20] United Kingdom	Argentina Austria Brazil Chile Colombia Costa Rica Czech Republic Denmark France Georgia Greece Hungary	Iceland Ireland Italy Israel The Netherlands New Zealand Norway Spain Sweden Switzerland[21] United States	
Boat Registry	Argentina Australia Austria Brazil Canada Czech Republic Denmark France Georgia Germany Greece	Honduras Iceland Ireland Japan Korea Mexico New Zealand South Africa Switzerland[22] United Kingdom United States	Colombia Costa Rica Hungary Israel Italy The Netherlands Norway	Spain Switzerland[23]	Chile

1. Written certified copies of documents from the Commercial Register.
2. Electronic certificate of incorporation, without official verification for operational purposes.
3. Some jurisdictions may not have such registry.
4. For designated officials in charge of tax crime investigations. Non-designated officials should manage their requests via SPPO.
5. The investigative authority has direct access to only 4 databases; access to any other tax database must be requested.
6. FPD, FIU.
7. FTA, CTA.
8. For designated officials in charge of tax crime investigations. Non-designated officials should manage their requests via SPPO.
9. YEDDE.
10. FTA.
11. YEDDE.
12. FCA.
13. Direct access to the criminal records database.
14. FPD, FIU.
15. SECA.
16. Request or spontaneous from the FIU.
17. YEDDE, FPD.
18. FIU.
19. The list of accounts held by a person is accessible on direct access, but not its balance or transactions, which are only accessible on request.
20. FTA, CTA.
21. FCA.
22. FTA, CTA.
23. FCA.

Principle 7 Make tax crimes a predicate offence for money laundering

Jurisdictions should designate tax crimes as one of the predicate offences for money laundering.

Introduction

100.   The FATF Recommendations provide that: "…Countries should apply the crime of money laundering to all serious offences, with a view to including the widest range of predicate offences" (Recommendation 3) (FATF, 2012-2020[1]).

101.   A predicate offence is a crime that is a component of a more serious crime. In regards to money laundering, predicate offences may give rise to funds or assets that may then be laundered to obscure the illegal source. For example, the predicate offence of drug trafficking can generate revenue, and through one of the basic steps of placement, layering and integration, conceal the illegal source of the funds, allowing the drug trafficker to use the funds without generating suspicion of criminal activity.[1]

102.   The designation of certain crimes as predicate offences means that a person can be charged with the offence of money laundering as well as with the predicate offence itself.

103.   During the latest revision of the FATF Recommendations, "tax crimes (related to direct and indirect taxes)" were separately identified in the existing list of specific categories of offences that should be predicate offences for money laundering (FATF, 2012-2020[1]).[2]

104.   Including tax crimes as a predicate offence for money laundering is important because it means that:

- A person that has committed money laundering can also be charged with the underling predicate offence. This may allow the authorities greater scope to secure a conviction and / or to impose greater penalties. In practice, whether the investigation or prosecution of one or both offences are pursued will depend on the case and factors such as the nature of the evidence and the elements of the offence which must be proven.

- Financial institutions and other designated professionals and reporting entities are required to file suspicious transaction reports (STRs), which report suspicions that a client's funds are the proceeds of a criminal activity, including money laundering as well as predicate offences. As such, STRs can include suspicions of where a client's funds are the proceeds of tax crimes. This can provide greater intelligence from the private sector to the government authorities. In order for this to be more effective, awareness of the risks and indicators of funds being the proceeds of tax crimes is needed amongst the relevant reporting entities. These reports are filed with the financial intelligence unit (FIU).

- STRs are analysed by the FIU and, where relevant, intelligence is disseminated to the domestic competent authorities responsible for investigating and / or prosecuting the relevant predicate offence. As such, it is possible for STRs to be shared by the FIU with the authority responsible for investigating and / or prosecuting tax crimes (OECD, 2015[2]) (See also Principle 8).[3]

- The mechanisms for international co-operation under the FATF Recommendations apply as between authorities that have responsibility for investigating and or prosecuting money laundering and predicate offences. Where tax crimes are included as predicate offences, those avenues for international co-operation are expanded to include authorities responsible for investigating and / or prosecuting tax crimes. This includes direct exchange of information and mutual legal assistance, both between tax investigatory and prosecution authorities and between tax and non-tax investigatory and prosecution authorities (see also Principle 9).

105.   In practice, virtually all jurisdictions surveyed have noted that the inclusion of tax crimes as a predicate offence has had a practical and positive impact on their work. Based on survey data, the most reported impact of tax crimes being a predicate offence was better inter-agency co-operation. This included increased ability to work with other agencies on particular cases and more generally on strategic and policy matters, more awareness amongst other law enforcement, intelligence agencies and amongst the private sector of the possibility of tax crimes occurring, and better avenues for communication with other agencies. Many jurisdictions also reported having better access to information (particularly from the FIU and increased STRs). Some jurisdictions also reported that prosecutions were easier to undertake and that there was an increase in prosecutions.

106.   Although "tax crimes" is not defined, the FATF Interpretive Note to Recommendation 3 states that jurisdictions are required to apply the crime of money laundering to all serious offences, with a view to including the widest range of predicate offences. Each jurisdiction must determine how the requirement will be implemented in their domestic law, including how it will define the offence and the elements of those offences that make them serious offences.

107.   There are different ways for jurisdictions to designate tax crimes as predicate offences for money laundering. For example, jurisdictions may:

- use an **inclusive approach** and identify all criminal offences as predicate offences;

- use a **threshold approach** and designate as a predicate offence all offences meeting a certain threshold, such as being punishable by one year imprisonment or more, or offences designated in a category of "serious offences;" or

- use a **list approach** and create an explicit list of offences that are predicate offences.

108.   All surveyed jurisdictions with the exception of Honduras have designated tax crimes as predicate offences for money laundering. Jurisdictions are using the following approaches in practice:

Figure 7.1. Approach to including tax crimes as a predicate offence for money laundering

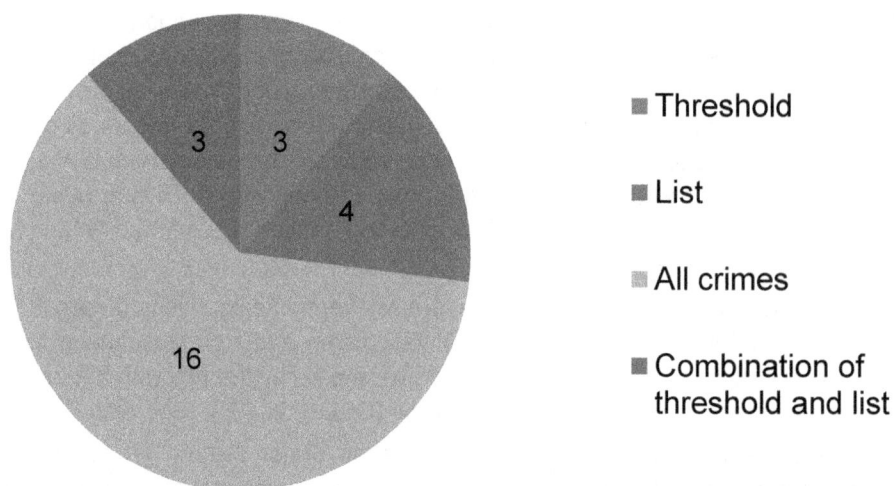

Note: **Threshold**: Australia, Austria, Canada; **List**: Colombia, Germany, Israel, Korea; **Combination**: Greece, Japan, Switzerland; **All crimes**: Argentina, Brazil, Czech Republic, France, Georgia, Hungary, Iceland, Ireland, Italy, Netherlands, New Zealand, Norway, South Africa, Spain, Sweden, United Kingdom.

109.   Three jurisdictions reported using the "threshold approach" (alone or as part of a combination of approaches). Some of these defined the threshold as offences punishable by a prison term exceeding a certain time (ranging from six months to four years) and others defined the threshold as those offences prosecuted by indictment.

References

FATF (2012-2020), *International Standards on Combating Money Laundering and the Financing of Terrorism & Proliferation*, FATF, http://www.fatf-gafi.org/publications/fatfrecommendations/documents/fatf-recommendations.html.   [1]

OECD (2015), *Improving Co-operation between Tax and Anti-Money Laundering Authorities*, OECD Publishing, https://www.oecd.org/tax/crime/improving-cooperation-between-tax-and-anti-money-laundering-authorities.htm.   [2]

Notes

[1] See also OECD (2009), *Money Laundering Awareness Handbook for Tax Examiners and Tax Auditors*, OECD Publishing, Paris, www.oecd.org/ctp/crime/money-laundering-awarenss-handbook.htm.

[2] The list of designated categories of offence included in the FATF Recommendations are: participation in an organised criminal group and racketeering; terrorism, including terrorist financing; trafficking in human beings and migrant smuggling; sexual exploitation, including sexual exploitation of children; illicit trafficking in narcotic drugs and psychotropic substances; illicit arms trafficking; illicit trafficking in stolen and other goods; corruption and bribery; fraud; counterfeiting currency; counterfeiting and piracy of products; environmental crime; murder, grievous bodily injury; kidnapping, illegal restraint and hostage-taking; robbery or theft; smuggling (including in relation to customs and excise duties and taxes); tax crimes (related to direct taxes and indirect taxes); extortion; forgery; piracy; and insider trading and market manipulation.

[3] See also principle 8 for more details and OECD, (2015), *Improving Co-operation between Tax and Anti-Money Laundering Authorities: Access by tax administrations to information held by financial intelligence units for criminal and civil purposes*, OECD, Paris, http://www.oecd.org/tax/crime/improving-co-operation-between-tax-and-anti-money-laundering-authorities.htm.

Principle 8 Have an effective framework for domestic inter-agency co-operation

Jurisdictions should have an effective legal and administrative framework to facilitate collaboration between tax authorities and other domestic law enforcement and intelligence agencies.

Introduction

110. Combating financial crimes comprises a number of key stages, including the prevention, detection, investigation and prosecution of offences, as well as the recovery of the proceeds of crime. Depending upon the circumstances, this can involve a number of government agencies, including the tax administration, the customs administration, financial regulators, AML authorities including the FIU, the police and specialised law enforcement agencies, anti-corruption authorities and the public prosecutor's office.

111. Furthermore, the various agencies may each have unique information or investigative and enforcement powers that can enhance another agency's investigation of a particular crime. This makes co-operation amongst the relevant agencies particularly important and beneficial. This includes information sharing, as well as other forms of co-operation. The forms of co-operation described below can also be used in parallel with each other, and one does not necessarily exclude the other. In order to make the best use of co-operation, it will be particularly helpful if the relevant agencies have identifiable contact points for information sharing and co-operation, as well as a clear understanding of the types of information and powers the other agencies possess.

112. Any such co-operation is subject to the domestic law and the need to prevent any abuse of powers, which is further discussed below. In addition, depending on the organisational structure in place in a

jurisdiction, and which agency has responsibility for investigating tax crimes different forms of co-operation may be appropriate (see Principle 5 for more details).

Information sharing

113.   A common form of co-operation is information sharing. In the course of their activities, different government agencies collect and hold information on individuals, corporations and transactions which may be directly relevant to the activities of other agencies in combating financial crime.

114.   Effective information sharing can be used to improve the prevention and detection of crimes, identify evidence which may lead to new investigations, and support ongoing investigations. In some cases information may be of a type that the receiving agency could not obtain directly, particularly where the information is of a specialist nature such as that held by the tax administration or FIU. In other cases, the ability to receive information from other agencies may reduce the duplication of work by different agencies, increasing the speed and reducing the cost of investigations, resulting in faster and more successful prosecutions, and increasing the likelihood of the proceeds of crime being recovered.

115.   In addition, sharing of information can be used to identify new avenues for investigation, such as where an investigation into a tax offence reveals other criminal activity and money laundering. The use of information from different sources may increase officers' understanding of an issue or of the activities of a suspect, possibly increasing the effectiveness of enquiries. Importantly, mechanisms for sharing information may be used to develop relationships between agencies, and key individuals in those agencies, which can be beneficial in developing new and enhanced forms of inter-agency co-operation.

Legal gateways for information sharing

116.   In order for information to be shared, legal gateways must exist between the relevant agencies. Legal gateways for sharing information may take a number of forms:

- Primary legislation often provides the basic framework for co-operation. This could be by explicitly requiring that an agency shares certain types of information in specified circumstances, or by generally allowing information sharing between agencies subject to limited exceptions.

- Where permitted by law, agencies may enter into bilateral agreements or 'memoranda of understanding', agreeing to share information where this is of relevance to the other agency's activities. These memoranda typically contain details of the types of information that will be shared, the circumstances in which sharing will take place and any restrictions on sharing information such as that the information may only be used for specified purposes. Memoranda may also include other terms agreed by the agencies, such as the format of any request for information, details of competent officials authorised to deal with requests, and agreed notice periods and time limits or a requirement for the agency receiving information to provide feedback on the results of investigations in which the information was used.

Models of information sharing

117.   Generally, there are four different types of co-operation with respect to sharing information among different agencies:

- direct access to information contained in agency records or databases. This can include direct access to mass or bulk data as well as specific access rights to a particular case record or file;

- an obligation to provide information automatically (i.e. at regular intervals) or spontaneously (i.e. on the occasions when relevant information is identified), normally where the categories of such information are pre-defined (sometimes expressed as a 'reporting obligation');
- an ability, but not an obligation, to provide information spontaneously; and
- an obligation or ability to provide information but only in response to a specific request which is made on a case-by-case basis.

Forms of information sharing

118. Different forms of information sharing may be particularly effective in different contexts. For example:

- Where information is suitable for using analytics and high-level risk assessment, direct access, or automatic or spontaneous exchange could be most effective. Operationally, this will be most effective if the types of information to be shared are clearly defined and can be automated. It also can assist in the detection of previously unknown criminal activity. Training on using direct access mechanisms, including the protections and processes necessary to ensure confidentiality and data protection may be relevant in this case.
- Discretionary spontaneous sharing of information may be very effective when there is a long-standing co-operative relationship between the agencies involved, and there is a clear understanding of what information may be useful in the activities of the recipient agency. Like direct access or automatic exchange, this can assist in proactively alerting an agency to previously unknown criminal activity. This should at a minimum include spontaneous sharing of information by tax authorities with the appropriate domestic law enforcement authorities of suspicions of serious crimes, including foreign bribery, money laundering and terrorism financing. (OECD, 2009[1]) (OECD, 2010[2])
- Where the information needed is very specific or needs to be in a certain form, information on request or direct access to a specific case record may be most suitable. This is likely to be most relevant when an investigation is relatively well advanced and the investigating agency already has sufficient information to provide the basis of the request.

119. Given the range of investigative techniques available throughout the course of an investigation, it may be most effective if the broadest possible range of information sharing methods is available, both from and to the agency investigating tax crimes. However, whichever types of information sharing are used, it is important to protect the confidentiality of information and the integrity of work carried out by other agencies, and in accordance with domestic law. This would likely include setting clear parameters relating to which people can access the information and for what purpose, as well as having governance mechanisms in place to ensure information is used appropriately.

Other forms of co-operation

120. In addition to information sharing, there is a range of other forms of co-operation being used by law enforcement authorities, with a number of examples described below.

Joint investigation teams

121. These enable agencies with a common interest to work together in an investigation. In addition to sharing information, this enables an investigation team to draw on a wider range of skills and experience from investigators with different backgrounds and training. Joint investigations may avoid duplication

arising from parallel investigations, and increase efficiency by enabling officials from each agency to focus on different aspects of an investigation, depending upon their experience and legal powers. In some cases, gateways for sharing information are wider when agencies are engaged in a joint investigation than they would be in other circumstances.

Box 8.1. Australia's Serious Financial Crime Taskforce

The Serious Financial Crime Taskforce (SFCT), led by the Australian Taxation Office, is a joint-agency taskforce established on 1 July 2015. It brings together the knowledge, resources and experience of relevant law enforcement and regulatory agencies to identify and address the most serious and complex forms of financial crime. As such the SFCT is the primary mechanism utilised by the ATO to respond to serious financial crime.

Participating members of the SFCT include: Australian Federal Police (AFP), Australian Tax Office (ATO), Australian Criminal Intelligence Commission (ACIC), Attorney-General's Department (AGD), Australian Transaction Reports and Analysis Centre (AUSTRAC), Australian Securities and Investments Commission (ASIC), Commonwealth Director of Public Prosecutions (CDPP), Department of Home Affairs (Home Affairs), incorporating its operational arm, the Australian Border Force (ABF) and Services Australia.

The SFCT brings together the knowledge, resources and experiences of relevant law enforcement and regulatory agencies to identify and address serious crimes that present the highest risk to Australia's tax and superannuation system. It also supports Australia's involvement as a member the Joint Chiefs of Global Tax Enforcement (J5).

Inter-agency centres of intelligence

122.   These are typically established to centralise processes for information gathering and analysis for a number of agencies. Inter-agency centres may be established to focus on operational information (case-specific information and investigations) or strategic information (broader assessment of risks and threats, focusing on a specific geographic area or type of criminal activity, or having a wider role in information sharing). These centres conduct analysis based on primary research as well as information obtained by participating agencies. By centralising these activities, officials can obtain experience of particular legal and practical issues, and specialised systems can be developed which can increase their effectiveness. Cost savings may also be achieved, as the expense of collecting, processing and analysing data can be shared between participating agencies.

Secondments and co-location of personnel:

123.   This is an effective way of enabling skills to be transferred while allowing personnel to build contacts with their counterparts in another agency. Seconded officials share their skills, experience and specialist knowledge while participating directly in the work of the host agency. Jurisdictions report that arrangements to co-locate and second staff have wider benefits for inter-agency co-operation, including encouraging officials to recognise opportunities for co-operation, more proactive engagement with counterparts from other agencies, improving the effectiveness of co-operation that does take place, and increasing the speed and efficiency of information sharing.

Other models

124. Other strategies include the use of shared databases, dissemination of strategic intelligence products such as newsletters and intelligence briefs, joint committees to co-ordinate policy in areas of shared responsibility, and inter-agency meetings and training sessions to share information on trends in financial crime, guidance on investigative techniques and best practice in managing cases.

125. In the context of the above, particular areas where inter-agency co-operation has been successful in some jurisdictions include:

- Granting the tax administration access to STRs (or "suspicious activity reports") (OECD, 2015[3])
- Granting the FIU access to information held by the tax administration
- Having a co-ordinated strategy for analysing and responding to STRs
- Putting obligations on tax officials to report suspicions of non-tax crimes to the police or public prosecutor
- The use of multi-agency task forces to combat financial crimes
- Putting in place a centralised structure for inter-agency co-operation
- Developing a co-ordinated approach to recovering the proceeds of crime
- Co-operation with the private sector in the fight against tax crime.

126. For more information on models of inter-agency co-operation, see the OECD report on Effective Inter-Agency Co-operation in Fighting Tax Crimes and Other Financial Crimes of 2017. (OECD, 2017[4])

References

OECD (2017), *Effective Inter-Agency Co-Operation in Fighting Tax Crimes and Other Financial Crimes - Third Edition*, OECD Publishing, Paris, https://www.oecd.org/tax/crime/effective-inter-agency-co-operation-in-fighting-tax-crimes-and-other-financial-crimes.htm . [4]

OECD (2015), *Improving Co-operation between Tax and Anti-Money Laundering Authorities*, OECD Publishing, https://www.oecd.org/tax/crime/improving-cooperation-between-tax-and-anti-money-laundering-authorities.htm. [3]

OECD (2010), *Recommendation of the Council to Facilitate Co-operation between Tax and Other Enforcement Authorities to Combat Serious Crimes*, http://acts.oecd.org/Instruments/ShowInstrumentView.aspx?InstrumentID=266. [2]

OECD (2009), *Recommendation of the Council on Tax Measures for Further Combating Bribery of Foreign Public Officials in International Business Transactions*, https://www.oecd.org/tax/crime/2009-recommendation.pdf. [1]

Principle 9 Ensure international co-operation mechanisms are available

Tax crime investigation agencies must have access to criminal legal instruments and an adequate operational framework for effective international co-operation in the investigation and prosecution of tax crimes.

Introduction

127. Tax crimes very frequently have an international dimension, for instance because a foreign jurisdiction was used to hide assets or income, or because the proceeds from illicit transactions are kept abroad, without being declared to tax authorities. Since criminal activity can cross international borders while investigation agencies have powers which are limited by jurisdictional boundaries, co-operation amongst investigation agencies is extremely important.

128. International co-operation can take a number of forms including information sharing; service of documents; obtaining evidence; facilitating the taking of testimony from witnesses; transferring persons for questioning; executing freezing and seizing orders; and joint investigation. In order for such co-operation to take place, there should be a legal agreement setting out the terms and procedural requirements. These agreements can be information sharing agreements, such as tax information exchange agreements (TIEAs), agreements for exchange of information and administrative assistance, bilateral tax treaties and other instruments (such as the multilateral Convention on Mutual Administrative Assistance in Tax Matters)) as well as agreements for co-operation in using investigative and coercive powers (such as MLATs). These agreements should authorise international co-operation for crimes including tax crimes.

129. The use of exchange of information and MLATs amongst survey respondents is set out below. It is noted that in some cases, data was not broken down to exclude non-tax crime requests, and this is noted and shown in italics where relevant.

Table 9.1. Survey responses: Numbers of EOI and MLAT requests in respect of criminal tax matters (2015-18, unless otherwise stated)

Jurisdiction	EOI requests sent	EOI requests received	MLAT request sent	MLAT requests received
Argentina	162	25	14	N/A
Australia	1	4	736	706
Canada	48	8	10	N/A
Costa Rica	6	N/A	N/A	N/A
Czech Republic	N/A	N/A	9 691	N/A
France	N/A	N/A	79	29
Georgia	16	28	19	65
Germany	4 500	4 000	N/A	N/A
Hungary	2 398	985	528	1 204
Iceland	86	4	0	0
Ireland	N/A	N/A	23	68
Japan	2 430	901	27	N/A
Korea	456	380	N/A	N/A
Mexico	N/A	N/A	30	13
Netherlands	1	0	91	544
Spain	4 292	7 204	1 685	N/A
Switzerland	2	N/A	12	N/A
United Kingdom	N/A	N/A	384	N/A
United States	55	N/A	N/A	approximately 15

Note: Figures for Australia are for the 2015-16 period. Figures for the Czech Republic are for the 2017-19 period and include all criminal offences. Figures for France are for the 2017-18 period and only concern MLA requests regarding non-EU jurisdictions (requests from within the EU are handled directly by the courts). Figures for Germany are approximate and for the 2011-19 period. Figures for Ireland are for the 2015-19 period on requests sent, and for the 2015-17 period for requests received. Figures for Hungary are for the 2015-19 period and only include requests for international assistance sent or received by NTCA, not HFIU. Figures for Korea are for the 2017-19 period and include both tax and criminal matters. Figures for the Netherlands are for the 2015-17 period. Figures for Spain are for the 2016-18 period. Figures for Switzerland are for the 2015-16 period. Figures for the United Kingdom are for the 2017-19 period and are only valid for England and Wales. Figures for the United States are for the 2015-16 period.

130.   With a view to having a successful holistic approach to fighting tax crime, it is important that jurisdictions have a far-reaching and functioning international co-operation network. This network should be characterised by the following features:

- be in place with a wide geographical coverage of other jurisdictions;

- cover a wide range of types of assistance, including exchange of information and other forms of assistance in investigation and enforcement; (OECD, 2012[1])

- be supported by a domestic legal framework that allows the sharing of information both sent and received under international legal instruments with all relevant domestic criminal investigation, intelligence and enforcement agencies, where appropriate (i.e. tax authorities, criminal investigation authorities, FIUs, AML authorities); and

- be given effect in practice, including having a clear operational framework for international co-operation. This should include having dedicated and identified contact points that foreign agencies can contact in case of a request for assistance, sufficient resources to fulfil requests for assistance, as well as training and awareness for domestic investigation agencies as to the availability of international co-operation and how to make effective requests.

131.   Although the legal gateways are in place in many cases, practical obstacles can have a significant impact on effective international co-operation. Surveyed jurisdictions reported obstacles such as: delays caused by a lack of clear communication channels, confusion about the organisational structure or mandate in the counterpart and therefore delays in identifying the correct agency to whom to address the request, and practical communication difficulties including language or lack of clarity in the presentation of the facts of the request. Results from the survey conducted for this guide also showed that jurisdictions may not keep detailed data to monitor the use or impact of the international co-operation tools, which may contribute to a lack of awareness or reduced profile of these tools.

References

OECD (2012), *International Co-operation against Tax Crimes and Other Financial Crimes: A Catalogue of the Main Instruments*, https://www.oecd.org/ctp/crime/international-co-operation-against-tax-crimes-and-other-financial-crimes-a-catalogue-of-the-main-instruments.htm.   [1]

Principle 10 Protect suspects' rights

Taxpayers suspected or accused of committing a tax crime must be able to rely on basic procedural and fundamental rights.

Introduction

132.	Persons subject to a criminal tax investigation should be able to rely on certain procedural and fundamental rights, which are afforded to everyone suspected or accused of a criminal act, including tax crime.

133.	The United Nations' Universal Declaration of Human Rights sets out the fundamental human rights which are to be universally protected (United Nations, 1948[1]). Similar rights and guidelines can for instance be found in the European Convention on Human Rights (European Court of Human Rights, Council of Europe, 1950-2010[2]) and the African Commission on Human & Peoples' Rights, Principles and Guidelines on the Right to a Fair Trial and Legal Assistance in Africa (African Commission on Human and Peoples' Rights, 2003[3]). These rights may be given effect in domestic law by being enshrined in a jurisdiction's constitution or bill of rights, or within criminal procedure law (US Government, 2002[4]) (Government of Canada, 2021[5]).

134.	In particular, taxpayers suspected or accused of committing a tax crime should be able to rely on the following rights:

- The right to a presumption of innocence;
- The right to be advised of their rights;
- The right to be advised of the particulars of what one is accused of;
- The right to remain silent;
- The right to access and consult a lawyer and entitlement to free legal advice;
- The right to interpretation and translation;

- The right to access documents and case material, also known as a right to full disclosure;
- The right to a speedy trial; and
- The right to protection from double jeopardy (ne bis in idem).

135.   The criminal tax investigation agency needs to be aware of these fundamental rights since failure to do so will not only negatively impact on the rights of an individual, but may have an adverse effect on an investigation and prosecution of a tax crime, for example, where evidence obtained becomes inadmissible if the individual's rights were violated.

136.   In particular, as there are instances where a criminal investigation may have originated as an ordinary civil examination or audit procedure, jurisdictions should have safeguards to ensure that the rights of an accused are protected when there is a change from administrative to criminal law. For example, in a civil examination, the taxpayer has an obligation to provide information to the tax administration; however in a criminal investigation, the suspect may have the right to remain silent. This issue is of particular importance for tax administrations which direct and conduct criminal investigations within the same organisational structure as the civil tax (audit) function, referred to as organisational Model 1 in Principle 4 above.

137.   The line that separates a civil tax matter from a criminal tax matter can require judgement and may be unclear. Based on the survey, most jurisdictions reported that a civil investigation becomes a criminal investigation when there is a reasonable suspicion that a crime had been committed, or where the facts indicate that a crime may have been committed. A smaller number of jurisdictions use an objective marker to determine when a civil matter becomes a criminal investigation, and which is based on a threshold of the amount of tax evaded. Based on survey data, 11 jurisdictions reported that civil and criminal investigations cannot run in parallel, and in practice the civil / administrative tax audits would be suspended and the criminal investigation would take precedence. 19 jurisdictions reported the possibility for civil / administrative tax audits to be conducted in parallel with criminal investigations. Many of these added that there are safeguards to ensure that the rights of an accused are protected when there is a parallel civil and criminal investigation, such as ensuring the investigations are run independently.

138.   More detail on each of the rights of suspects is set out below.

The right to a presumption of innocence

139.   This is the principle that a person is considered innocent until proven guilty and it is a critical component of the criminal justice system. The presumption of innocence means the burden of proof is on the prosecution and not on the accused.

140.   As an example of how this can be implemented, the European Council recently adopted a directive to strengthen certain aspects of the presumption of innocence (European Council, 2016[6]). This Directive requires member states to respect the following related obligations: "before the final judgement, suspects and accused persons should not to be presented as being guilty through the use of measures of physical restraint and the burden of proof is on the prosecution while any reasonable doubts as to the guilt should benefit the accused."

The right of the suspect or accused to be advised of their rights

141.   This right places a duty on the investigating agency to advise a suspect or accused of their rights. In some jurisdictions, this obligation may be fulfilled by orally advising the person of their rights or in writing by issuing a "Letter of Rights". These rights will generally include the right to remain silent, the right to be informed of the accusations against the person and the right to access a lawyer or in some circumstances

the right to free legal advice. For example, in the United States this is known as a "Miranda Warning," and many other jurisdictions have equivalents (The Law Library of Congress, 2016[7]).

142.   In practice, jurisdictions may administer these rights at different stages of an investigation. Some jurisdictions advise an accused of their rights at the commencement of any questioning, while others may do so when a person is arrested.

The right to remain silent

143.   This is the right of an accused person to refuse to comment or provide answers when questioned by a criminal investigator. This right is recognised by most legal systems and protects an individual from self-incrimination. This right usually applies both prior to and during a trial.

The right to be advised of the particulars of what one is accused of

144.   This right enables the accused to know the nature and substance of the allegations against them. This would generally include the elements of the offence, such as the essential aspects of the offence, details of the alleged conduct which led to the charge and in the case of a tax crime, the alleged damage to the state. Generally, the particulars must be provided to an accused prior to the accused entering a plea in court.

The right to access and consult a lawyer and entitlement to free legal advice

145.   Someone accused of having committed a tax crime must have the opportunity to seek legal advice. In addition, if the accused cannot afford legal advice or legal representation, then there may be a right to state-funded legal assistance. This fundamental right is essential to a fair legal system, given the potentially serious consequences of a conviction.

146.   The specific details of these rights vary from jurisdiction to jurisdiction. Jurisdictions may have different practices with respect to when the right to seek legal advice becomes available. For example, in Canada the right extends to someone who has been detained or arrested. Jurisdictions will also have different approaches to the right to state-funded legal representation, which may be available only in specific circumstances such as where the accused meets certain financial criteria.

147.   In Europe, Article 6(3)(c) of the European Convention on Human Rights provides that a person charged with a criminal offence has the right "to defend himself in person or through legal assistance of his own choosing or, if he has not sufficient means to pay for legal assistance, to be given it free when the interests of justice so require" and this right may be applied both at the pre-trial stage and during the trial.

The right to interpretation and translation

148.   This right allows an accused person to understand the information about the criminal proceedings in their own language. This ensures that language barriers are not an obstacle to receiving a fair trial. The costs associated with these services are usually borne by the prosecuting authority.

149.   Generally this right should apply to the questioning of the suspect or accused by a representative of the state authority, meetings between the prosecution and the accused and their lawyer, and during all court appearances and hearings.

150.   For example, within the European Union, these rights extend to the translation of essential documents, including any decision depriving a person of his or her liberty, any charge or indictment and any judgment.

The right to access documents and case material, also known as a right to full disclosure

151.   This means that the accused has the right to know the details of the case which is argued against them, including the evidence held by the prosecutor. This allows the accused the opportunity to prepare a defence. This disclosure can also encourage the resolution of the case before going to a trial, such as encouraging an accused to confess to the crime and plead guilty.

152.   The way jurisdictions implement this right will vary. In some jurisdictions there is a duty on the prosecutor to provide disclosure of all evidence to an accused person, including evidence that is favourable to the accused and evidence that is favourable to the prosecution. This may be subject to the prosecutor's discretion with respect to timing and withholding information for valid reasons such as protection of an informant.

The right to a speedy trial

153.   This right should protect an accused person from undue delay in the resolution of a trial. This is because undue delay may:

- Prejudice the accused person from receiving a fair trial because evidence may become unavailable or less reliable. For example, the memory of a witness may become weak over time or witnesses may die.
- If the accused person is in prison pending the outcome of the trial, he or she may be imprisoned for an unreasonably lengthy period if t subsequently found not guilty of the crimeor if the sentence imposed on the accused is less than the time already served in prison.

154.   There may not be a definitive measurement of what is or is not a speedy trial and it may depend on several factors. In determining whether a breach of the right to a speedy trial has occurred, relevant factors may include:

- The length of the delay from the time the accused was charged with the crime until the case is tried;
- The reasons for the delay, including the complexity of completing the work necessary for the case to tried, delays caused by the defence, delays caused by the prosecution, institutional delays such as limited availability of trial dates in the relevant court, and other reasons for delay;
- Whether the accused has waived any delay; and
- The prejudice to the accused in terms of a fair trial, such as the impact on the availability or reliability of evidence.

The right to protection from ne bis in idem (double jeopardy)

155.   This right protects an accused of being tried twice for the same crime, where the person has previously been found guilty and served their sentence or the person has been acquitted by a final judgement. This also protects an accused from being tried again for a less serious crime, where all of the elements of that less serious crime are subsumed in the elements of the more serious crime. However,

this right does not prevent successive investigations where one investigation may not have resulted in criminal charges, but a subsequent investigation is commenced which is based on new evidence.

156.   The survey conducted shows that these rights are almost universally granted. The availability of these rights amongst surveyed jurisdictions is shown in the following chart.

Figure 10.1. Availability of suspects rights in tax offence cases

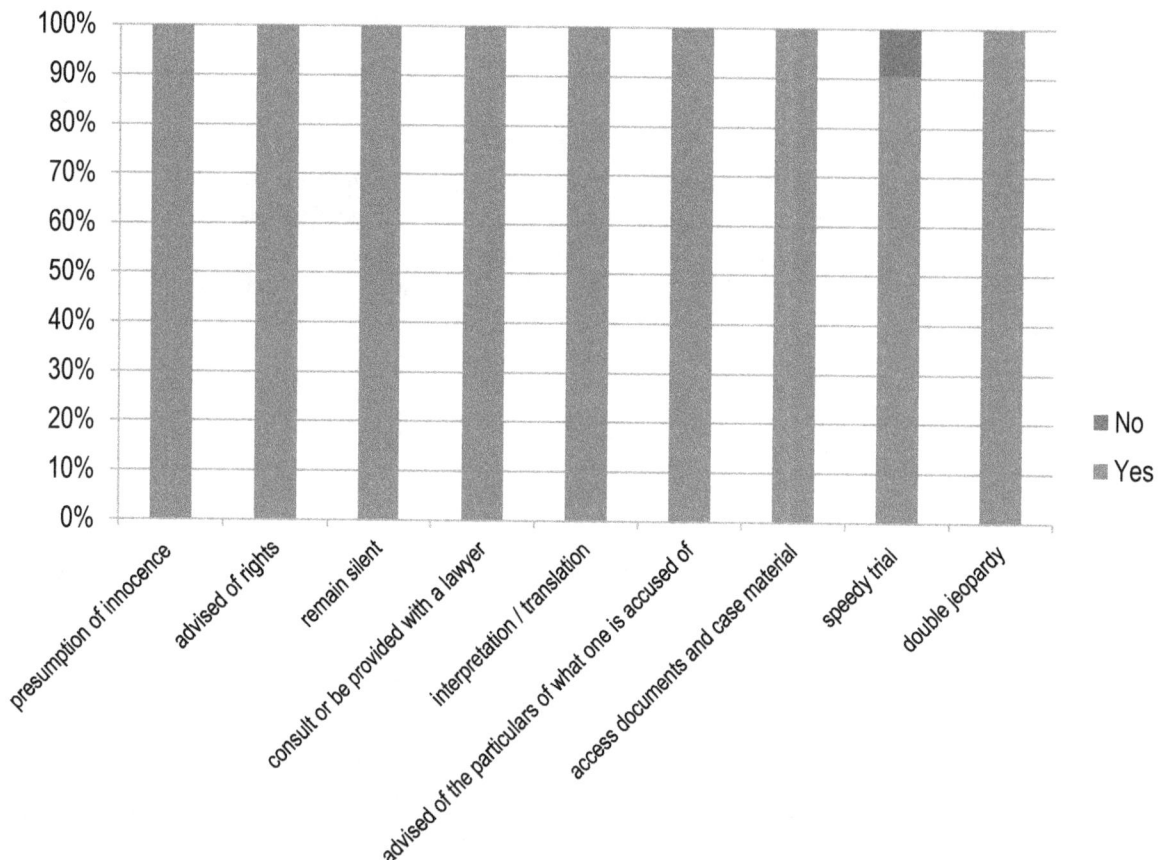

References

African Commission on Human and Peoples' Rights (2003), *Principles and Guidelines on the Right to a Fair Trial and Legal Assistance in Africa*, African Union, http://www.achpr.org/files/instruments/principles-guidelines-right-fair-trial/achpr33_guide_fair_trial_legal_assistance_2003_eng.pdf. [3]

European Council (2016), *Press realease and statement - EU Strengthens right to the presumption of innocence*, European Union, https://www.consilium.europa.eu/en/press/press-releases/2016/02/12/eu-strengthens-right-to-presumption-of-innocence/ (accessed on 19 April 2021). [6]

European Court of Human Rights, Council of Europe (1950-2010), *European Convention on Human Rights*, https://www.echr.coe.int/documents/convention_eng.pdf (accessed on 19 April 2021). [2]

Government of Canada (2021), *The Canadian Charter of Rights and Freedoms*, Minister of Justice of Canada, https://laws-lois.justice.gc.ca/eng/const/page-12.html#h-45 (accessed on 19 April 2021). [5]

The Law Library of Congress (2016), *Miranda Warning Equivalents Abroad*, Global Legal Research Center, https://www.loc.gov/law/help/miranda-warning-equivalents-abroad/miranda-warning-equivalents-abroad.pdf. [7]

United Nations (1948), *The Universal Declaration of Human Rights*, https://www.un.org/en/about-us/universal-declaration-of-human-rights (accessed on 19 April 2020). [1]

US Government (2002), *Sixth Amendment - Rights of Accused in Criminal Prosecutions*, https://www.govinfo.gov/content/pkg/GPO-CONAN-2002/pdf/GPO-CONAN-2002-9-7.pdf (accessed on 19 April 2021). [4]

Annex A. List of participating jurisdictions in the 2nd edition of the Ten Global Principles

While the intention is that this report will stay as an open document, available for any jurisdiction willing to participate in the benchmarking exercise in the future, the statistics and successful case studies in this edition were last updated in April 2021. The list below details the name of each participating jurisdiction in alphabetical order, and the agency which acted as point of contact for discussing the contents of their respective country chapters with the Secretariat.

1. Argentina: Federal Administration of Public Revenue (AFIP)
2. Australia: Australian Taxation Office
3. Austria: Federal Ministry of Finance (BMF)
4. Azerbaijan: State Secretariat of Taxes
5. Brazil: Federal Revenue of Brazil (RFB)
6. Canada: Canada Revenue Agency – Criminal Investigations Directorate
7. Chile: Internal Taxes Service (SII)
8. Colombia: Directorate for National Taxes and Customs (DIAN)
9. Costa Rica: Ministry of the Treasury
10. Czech Republic: Ministry of Finance
11. Estonia: Investigations Department of the Estonian Tax and Customs Board
12. France: General Directorate of Public Finances (DGFiP)
13. Georgia: Investigations Service of the Ministry of Finance
14. Germany: Federal Ministry of Finance (BMF)
15. Greece: Independent Authority of Public Revenue (AADE)
16. Honduras: Tax Crime Unit of the Income Administration Service (SAR)
17. Hungary: Criminal Directorate of the National Tax and Customs Administration
18. Iceland: Directorate of Tax Investigations
19. Ireland: Revenue Commissioners
20. Israel: Israel Tax Authority
21. Italy: *Guardia di Finanza* and Ministry of Economy and Finance
22. Japan: Criminal Investigations Division of the National Tax Agency
23. Korea: National Tax Service
24. Mexico: Tax Prosecution Agency of the Federation (PFF)
25. Netherlands: Fiscal Information and Investigation Service (FIOD)
26. New Zealand: Inland Revenue
27. Norway: Tax Administration
28. South Africa: South African Revenue Service

29. Spain: Spanish Agency of Tax Administration (AEAT)
30. Sweden: Tax Administration
31. Switzerland: Federal Tax Administration
32. United Kingdom: Her Majesty's Revenue and Customs
33. United States: Internal Revenue Service – Criminal Investigations

Annex B. Country chapters

The country chapters detail jurisdictions' domestic tax crime enforcement frameworks as well as the progress made in implementing the Ten Global Principles. These reports are available separately at the OECD website at: https://www.oecd.org/tax/crime/fighting-tax-crime-the-ten-global-principles-second-edition-country-chapters.pdf